I0706594

EVERYTHING
THE GOVERNMENT DOES
IS BAD FOR US

By Ryan Aleckszander

Written in 2021
Spring, Texas,
USA

Cover art by Ryan Aleckszander

1. More Than Failure.

I often find myself going easy on the government. I let them off the hook by attributing the consequences of their actions to a *failure*.

In this book, I will not be so kind. I believe that the results of government policies and actions are *more* than mere failure. Whichever country we are talking about, I believe all government policies and actions are actively harmful.

Yes, all of them.

Failure presumes a level of innocence, ignorance, or accident. I do not believe these excuses are justified. Governments do know what they are doing. Modern policies all have long histories and precedents. We are not experimenting – these are tried and true procedures.

They haven't just failed us, they have harmed us. And they will continue to do so unless we make dramatic changes in our government systems.

We have had more than enough time to see the consequences of every government policy. There is no longer any excuse for the pain and suffering these policies continue to cause.

All policy derives first from ideology. The people who comprise governments believe certain things, and they form policies around these beliefs. I will argue that these ideologies are flawed at the core, and so any policies derived from them will also be flawed.

There are two parts to my grievances with the government. First, we do not need the government to do the things it does. The useful functions we supposedly need the government to oversee can be handled by private enterprises. Often, these functions are already contracted privately. Roads are built and maintained by private companies, schools can be run privately just as effectively as by the government, and every other aspect of the amenities that comprise our modern life can be designed, built, and regulated by private industries.

The second grievance is that governments tend to do things that do not need to be done at all.

In the first case, the harm is a simple waste of resources. We do not need the middleman to contract private businesses. In the second case, the harm is much greater. When governments take it upon themselves to impose unnecessary rules, infrastructure, propaganda campaigns, and wars, we are all harmed.

In my lifetime I have considered myself both a liberal and a conservative. I have voted for both left and right parties in my home country. I am now convinced that the distinction between left and right is a false dichotomy. These are two heads of the same serpent.

I will not make the case that we should abolish government outright. We have a society deeply structured around an existing control system. Removing the system completely, I do believe would be chaos.

I think there is a way out, but we must first understand the problem before we can really talk about a solution.

2. Roads & Infrastructure.

If you've ever wondered out loud about why we actually need governments, somebody near you probably responded that we at least need them to build roads and other essential infrastructure.

Interestingly, roads existed before the taxes that are said to have paid for them. I don't really know what happened back in Roman times, but I do know that our modern road systems were not built directly by governments.

In different countries, states, and municipalities, there are different ratios of different taxes diverted to pay for roads. The problem here is, the government does not actually build the road. The government takes your money, whether from a "gas tax", or income tax, or some other tax, and they use your money to pay a private company to build a road.

Here I am talking about non-communist governments. Communist governments will probably completely control the infrastructure building. It is not necessary for a communist government to build a road if private enterprise is perfectly capable of building roads. And life in a communist country is arguably much worse than the mild "democratic" governments we will focus on in this book. Living under totalitarian rule is too high a price to pay for roads.

Anarchy as a political concept is essentially just the absence of government. The basic anarchist answer to who would build the roads is something like: people who want roads, will build the roads.

I must admit that this answer does not satisfy me.

My friend has a private property with a very rudimentary road on it. It is so rough that most vehicles can't make it 20 feet without getting stuck. We have considered various types of landscaping and construction to make the property more accessible, each of which is extremely expensive in the final analysis.

To this day we do not have a proper road on the property. This is fine because there is no dire need. There is no community dependent on this potential infrastructure, and ultimately a road would not change that much. It would make our lives a little bit easier, and that is all. This is not enough of a reason to justify any major construction project.

My house is in a town called Kirkland Lake, in northern Ontario, Canada. The roads in my town are terrible. I can't think of one road that is in good shape. In front of our house is a nature-made speed bump, and at all hours we periodically hear the double thump of an unsuspecting vehicle learning about it.

Kirkland Lake is a company town. The Kirkland Lake Gold mining company is the largest employer, and thus the largest tax contributor. The town is responsible for all of the roads except one. Though the town is technically in control, I do not really consider the town administration to be "the government." The real government presence in town are provincial police and other provincial offices for licenses and passports.

The one road that crosses through the town and connects us with towns to the east and west, is owned and managed by the province of Ontario. This road is called Government Road, and I have to admit that it is the nicest road in town.

Since this road is owned by the province, it is designated as a "highway." I'm sure there are some exceptions, but generally the roads in Canada are the responsibility of municipalities, while longer roads called highways are the responsibility of the province or the federal government.

Our town, like many small towns, is run very much like a small business. A portion of the revenue generated by the town economy is diverted to things like roads, water systems, and street lights. The small size of the town is probably the main reason why the local government has a hard time wasting a lot of money.

There are very few town employees, and they live among the common people. If they screw up, the people will show up to tell them how they feel. The people who run the town are neighbors and friends with the regular people. This keeps the administration in town largely *accountable* for their actions.

Our town is small enough where nearly every budget concern is openly debated in town hall meetings. In northern Canada, we only have two main seasons: winter, and construction season. Every year the town gets together and talks about which roads are the priority for this year's construction season.

I like this system. There has never been a totally extravagant waste of money from the town budget, as far as I can tell. This does not exactly fit my dramatic title for this book, but we must start somewhere.

Northern Canada has a particularly hard task with maintaining roads. There are very old roads in California that are in much better shape than quite new roads in Canada. The extreme temperature fluctuations between winter and summer ensure that roads in our cold country require constant attention.

None of this justifies government control of the roads. We pay property taxes for our slices of the town. Those taxes are pooled for the town to distribute into projects such as roads, water, and snow removal. In our small town this is a fairly efficient system, but there are some odd concepts that arise with this government jurisdiction.

For one, residents themselves are not allowed to intervene with the road. This makes a certain level of sense – in many places such as New York City, if people did try to dig, practically anywhere, they are very likely to cause some kind of damage to a buried pipe or cable.

Official road workers often do this damage inadvertently. Professional responsibility does not completely mitigate the risk of someone screwing up a utility by trying to fix the road. These accidents still happen, but insurance is much easier to deal with when it is an official mistake.

This system makes less sense in much of the very large country of Canada, or the majority of the rural landmass of the United States and most other modern countries. The hazardous speed bump in front of my house is not supposed to be there, and while these types of decisions are readily made at local town meetings, there is still enough of these such bumps that my street has not been made a priority.

It would probably take a day of work, and a few thousand dollars of equipment and material for a small group of us to fix the bump. Realistically, we could probably fix it for free. My neighbors are mostly strong and capable men, and together we already own most of the tools we would need for the job. I'm sure I'm not the only one who is often woken up by the THUMP, THUMP, from a passing vehicle who didn't know there was a giant bump in the road. I'm sure at least a few of us would agree on a plan to fix the bump.

We are not allowed to fix the bump, because the government controls the road.

If any one of us attempted to smooth out the bump, or fill in a pothole, it is likely that a government employee will penalize us with a ticket. We could pay the ticket, or we could "fight" it, which would cost even more taxpayer money in the form of court employees having to see the case. The cost of any one of these litigious incidents would be greater than the cost to fix the bump.

There are some places where the roads are so bad that they're nearly impractical to drive on. One winter in Montreal essentially cost me a car. Some potholes in Michigan or Indiana – or anywhere in the Midwest, really – could swallow your family. These roads are supposed to be "handled" by the government, and yet they are handled exceptionally poorly.

The people of Michigan tell me that for a short time in living memory they had some of the finest roads in their nation. They were proud of their smooth and safe roads and they appreciated the tax system that afforded them this. A change in this tax distribution has left them with some of the most badly neglected roads in the industrialized world.[i] The excuse seems simply to be a lack of funding. Gas taxes are relatively high in Michigan compared to its neighboring states, and yet much of that is not spent on roads.

This example covers both of my problems with government: Governments often fail in their duty to provide good roads, which is simply a misuse or waste of tax money. And they also actively harm us when they litigate private attempts to take responsibility for bad roads. The punishment we get for attempting to make up for government mistakes costs us even more tax money.

If we had perfect roads, I would still have a problem. I would ask why we couldn't just pay for our roads ourselves. We have somewhat agreed to pay property taxes. It's not like we had a vote on that, but I don't hear much grumbling about it. I see no reason why we couldn't directly apportion some of that to contractors for road maintenance.

The organizations who currently build and maintain our roads are private companies. It is not "Canada Road Corporation" doing the digging and the filling, it is private construction companies. I see no reason why overpaid bureaucrats need to middleman this transaction.

If we paid for roads with property tax, or any other fundraising scheme, wouldn't it still be some form of government that ended up dealing with the money? Governments have many other functions than roads and infrastructure, and our taxes pay for all kinds of things that are not essential. Town budgets don't go to war and they don't have much or anything to do with most of this book. I would be fine with a government small enough where its only responsibilities were budgeting for essential matters.

Our small town has just over 100 lane kilometers of roads, and 2 bridges. This would not be difficult to contract out. There is very little need for any bean counting or tough decisions. The task of deciding which roads to fix first, based on our town budget, is not brain surgery. It does not require an elected official with a university degree or a government-employed engineer to oversee any of this.

Bigger towns have more roads and more bridges and so on. But the decisions don't get much more difficult than simply agreeing to pay this company X amount for the job. I agree with the anarchist's view that residents of individual municipalities, or even individual city blocks, are completely capable of overseeing this simple budgeting.

Without government interference, many simple problems could be fixed locally. We don't need formal contracts to fix many potholes and unintended speed bumps. Citizens could screw up a construction project, but so can companies. People tend to strive to do a good job, especially when it is right outside of their house. Those who are completely incompetent at fixing potholes are probably not going to be the first ones to volunteer for the job.

New housing or commercial developments typically have to construct their own smaller roads, parking lots, parking garages, and their own plumbing before it connects into the main system, and towns are already responsible for most of their roads. State, provincial, or federal governments are much more of my problem, and their involvement in roads is reduced mostly to highways.

I will admit that governments can indeed get things done. It seems that the more concentrated the power is and the less room for argument, the faster it is to approve of and begin construction on mega projects. Private industry would have a hard time keeping up with what governments are capable of. But I do believe that we can find solutions when things do need to be done.

This is a good time to bring up incentives.

I have many friends in the construction industry. When their contract comes from a private company, they tend to be under serious pressure to *keep the budget down*. When they pay for work, they want the cost to be *low as possible*, usually.

Private companies do not want to see workers standing around wasting time. They paid for the pothole in the parking lot to be fixed, and they expect it to be fixed efficiently, at which time the clock stops and the job is done. They do not want to pay for extra time or material. This sounds straightforward, but it is the exact opposite of what occurs under government contract.

Governments have incentives to *fill their budget*. A government department that does not spend its entire budget is unlikely to get the same budget next year. This is a *bad* thing for a government department. Everybody wants to keep their job, *and* see their salaries increase with time. Whether it is a police force or a school board, the motivation is to *spend the budget.* They want to spend it all, so they can justify asking for more next year.

Private companies and individuals want to finish the job *under budget.* You want your basement renovated for *less* than you thought it would cost, or at least, for as little money as possible. But if this was a government, that basement renovation department *risks* "losing" some of their budget next year if they do not spend their entire budget this year.

I repeated the point because it really is incredible. A company under contract to fix roads for a government *does not want to do the job as efficiently as possible.* If they work "too hard" and get the job done "too quickly", they lose bargaining power for the next contract. They want *more money* next year. This motivation exists for every government department, agency, and contractor.

Private companies are accountable to the market in general, and their investors specifically. The people who own stock in the company do not want them wasting time or money. They want material and labor costs as low as possible, so profit can be high as possible.

Say what you will about this system, but I find it much more appealing than the opposite – the incessant hunger for higher and higher annual budgets by every government department on Earth.

An argument might be put on the table here about quality. We don't want to cheap out on our roads, do we? No – we expect a certain standard of quality for our infrastructure.

The company who does the job more efficiently can still be held to the same market standard for quality. They will have to find other ways to keep the costs down that do not include lowering quality. Maybe they use more efficient materials. Maybe they cut administrative fat from their company to lower the overall operating costs. There are many paths to efficiency.

There are also many paths to inefficiency. When the government is paying for the job, workers can easily stand around and waste any "extra" time. They can stockpile "extra" material that the government "already paid for." Don't think this happens? Ask your construction friend.

I started with one of the least important responsibilities of the government because it is the most common objection to the concept of anarchy.

The truth is, in absence of government, there are still roads. They might not be the best roads in the world, but government contracts also do not guarantee great roads.

I would make a strong argument that the highest quality and best maintained roads exist on private properties. The finest roads I have ever driven on exist as part of private infrastructure such as airports, malls, and private communities.

Different locations have different needs and challenges for their infrastructure. We do not specifically require a government to face or finance any of these specific challenges. Governments can hire appropriate engineers and builders, or these same professionals can be hired privately.

When there is a need for roads, humans come together and figure it out. Often, maximum efficiency is prevented by governments, since they do not allow anyone other than their sanctioned companies to perform the work. These companies are incentivized to squeeze every possible dollar from the government, which really means from our tax purse.

Governments *can* get things done very quickly. They can pay for highways and bridges and sewers and more and these projects can be completed in reasonable time. Private companies can also get things done quickly, though when we are talking about roads we are entering a different business model from much of the existing construction industry.

Things are usually built for a purpose, and in private industry that purpose ultimately has to pay off. The people doing the building are usually not the people who will profit off of what is built – they are just paid to build the thing. When we build high rise condominiums and shopping plazas and airports and so on, whoever paid for the building has a clear plan to see a return on their investment.

For a private company to build a road, it has to have a plan of profit attached to it. Sometimes it is simple – people need to navigate around the shopping plaza, and the project justifies investments in some roads and parking space. Outside of the plaza or the airport or the housing complex, there is no profit for a private business to build or maintain a road, unless there is a toll.

I do think that tolls make sense on large, densely used roads. It is expensive to build and maintain large transport systems, especially in cities.

In a world without government, we may still have some taxes. We are already used to paying more for basically everything in dense cities, and this is a type of tax. It costs more to live and operate there, and every type of business tends to charge more. Cities could pool money from the many industries, cultural activities, business conferences, and anything else that generates money. This is just another form of tax, but it could be voluntary and wouldn't require a government to oversee the road contracting.

Since sales of everything go up and down, a more reliable generator of the money to build and maintain roads in cities and towns can come from a property tax. Cities will remain more expensive, and we can choose to live there or in cheaper places with less infrastructure.

If property tax were voluntary, there is a risk that a significant portion would not pay. This would not be fair to those who did pay. There is also a possibility that a significant portion *would* pay, and that they would generate enough to handle our basic needs. We might discover how *little* it costs to maintain our infrastructure compared with the old system.

If the roads were maintained I do doubt that the tax payers would feel grievance about the people who did not pay. Wealth and success concentrates in cities, and the people who will benefit most from paying what needs to be paid are the people who are already most invested in their businesses in those cities. They need good roads for their employees or customers to get to the business or factory.

These people in the current system would probably already have some grievances with the way tax money is spent, and who benefits from government assistance. These people are also already used to being taxed on everything, dealing with government inspectors and local permits and such that they would possibly end up paying much less if it were merely a property tax for essential infrastructure.

There is also the possibility of encouraging young people to sign up for volunteer road working and other civic functions. Training civilians for proper construction safety would be more time consuming than simply contracting whole projects out, but it might also be great for character building in the volunteers and they might discover a passion or distaste for the industry, in which case we have helped guide their career path. And they might actually be useful.

I volunteered at a gym as part of my final high school year and I learned a lot about gyms, and ended up working there for 4 years. Some of my friends did their volunteer hours in construction or trades, and several of them joined those trades as careers.

There are many jobs in any construction project that do not require touching a tool. The person who stands on the road and holds a stop sign to regulate traffic is a very important part of the team. I'm just brainstorming here, and combinations of any of these things are possible. A smaller government that does still handle "highways" is still progress to me. Property taxes staying local is better than it being spent somewhere else.

Energy:

In many countries it is illegal for you to harness your own power. If you opt for "renewable" energy sources, in most cases you are forced to feed this energy back into the grid.

The exception is usually for properties that are not already connected to a grid. So you can use a solar power setup at your cabin, but you cannot use a windmill or wood burner to generate electricity for your home, if that home is already connected to the grid. You must sell your power to your government, and buy some of their power back from the grid at a discounted price.

The government stops you from setting up a decentralized, efficient energy system. Unlike water, they do not attempt to say that this is for your own good – that's just how it is, just because they said so.

In Ontario, people who have bought or built alternative energy systems have been forced to feed that energy into the central grid, at a rate determined completely by the government. They receive a lower rate on the power they use personally, which comes from the same grid.

But Ontario already produces enough power. We actually export energy. There are 3 quite large nuclear facilities in the province that provide nearly 60% of electricity.[ii] Natural gas and water (Niagara Falls) are the next leading sources. Solar, wind, and other "renewables" have gone from less than 1% in 2005 to 9% in 2015, both because of market interest in "clean" technologies, and because of government programs dealing with the grid scheme.

If you didn't know how you can earn up to $_____ per year by installing this solar system on your roof, there is a sales force to tell you about it, and charge their fees to connect you with the government program. This scheme is similar in many other countries.

This entire initiative has largely been to produce energy we never needed, and is wasted. All this alternative energy infrastructure, encouraging citizens to invest and feed that energy into the grid, whole government departments created across the world for this purpose, and yet the Ontario Society of Professional Engineers spoke to a wall when they announced that as we have been increasing investment in alternative energy, the government has been increasing the amount of "clean energy" it wastes. In 2016 they apparently wasted enough energy to power every home in the province. Of course, during the time we have been producing more energy than we need, consumer prices for electricity continually increases.

I think this all happens because the government cares more about looking good through its programs than it does about those programs actually providing value. I am sure it also has to do with more solid government jobs created in all the new agencies and committees when these big ideas are brought forward.

Centralized energy production and distribution, from any source, involves incredibly massive waste. The infrastructure required to move around electricity from far away sources such as dams, nuclear plants, wind farms, or petroleum burning plants, is extraordinary. We must produce a lot more energy than we actually need, because more energy is wasted the farther it has to travel through the wires. Electricity also has to be supplied in higher voltage than we require at the point of use, because it has to travel such long distances.

Today, many of the devices we depend on for our modern conveniences – phones, tablets, GPS, handheld gaming systems, and so on – don't even require the AC (alternating current) that our grids apparently must run on. DC (direct current), wouldn't travel very far through the wires, so we must produce high voltage AC, which is stepped down to lower voltage to enter your town, and lower to enter your house, losing energy at each stage and with each unit of distance traveled. Any of that AC power is useless for all these devices that need constant charging, and so we have to plug them in through an adapter, which converts AC to DC, or to another DC device like a laptop computer.

Producing DC power is much easier than AC. A small solar panel can sit on the window and charge a battery pack, which you can plug several devices into. Besides communications and small entertainment devices, much of the lighting in a normal house could be DC powered. Small fans, garage door openers, coffee grinders, electric shavers, and many more small appliances can be DC. Larger things like refrigerators and heaters require more energy than is reliably given by a solar setup. The intermittency problem of solar and wind doesn't matter much when they are being used to charge battery packs for smaller devices.

We are told that we *must* use centralized types of energy systems, *because* we need to produce so much in order to supply us. This is a lie. We need massive infrastructure because the government insists on centralized energy production and distribution. Since we are forced to use a centralized system, we must build hugely wasteful energy transport systems in the form of power lines. Even the introduction of separate smaller systems for smaller applications moves us away from the centralized grid.

Sometimes this grid setup can be very strange. My town does not get its electricity from the power generating plant in our town. That plant sends the power off into the grid, while our town plugs into it. This is all worth the detail because there are major risks involved in a central power grid, on top of the wastes. If we were on a local power system, I have no doubt that there would be occasional outages in our harsh climate, and we are used to them already. But it would remain a local problem. Massive grids can affect massive groups of people when they malfunction, and this does happen.

In the winter of 2013 I was visiting my mother in Toronto, Ontario, when the city was hit with a once-in-a-lifetime ice storm. What really happened was a rainstorm that got cold very quickly. Trees were all wet, and when it froze quickly the weight of this ice brought down many branches.

The trees fell on the power lines, and there were so many of these all at once that it compromised the whole grid. Power was out for three days in some of the coldest temperatures known in the region. This never would have happened if it weren't for centralized energy delivered to homes via wooden sticks and wires. Some people would have been stuck in the cold either way, but if it weren't for the government many people would have had their own electricity.

This was the most dramatic civil unrest event I have ever witnessed, but it had almost nothing to do with the ice storm. The drama that ensued included hospitals without power, looting, people accidentally killing themselves by trying to stay warm with barbecues in the living room, and more. The power outage only happened because of the centralized energy system. All of this drama was due only to the power outage, and the whole mess was the government's fault. Ice storms are only a threat to silly centralized wires.

There was a similarly dramatic wide-scale power outage in 2003 which went down in history as the "Northeast Blackout." Power was out for 10 million people in southern and central Ontario, as well as 45 million people in 8 American states. The cause of this blackout is said to be a "software bug." 55 million people were without power for between 2 hours and 2 days. Widespread looting and other opportunistic crime ensued, though no one died from the cold because this happened in the summer.

This type of "software glitch" is impossible in a decentralized system, as such a glitch would never affect so many people if it weren't for a centralized energy system. This year (2021), in Texas, large-scale blackouts are also being blamed on the grid itself. The grid was not able to supply the increased demand, and it crashed.

This electricity system we are forced to plug into also often provides our heat, since our natural gas heating systems require electricity.

I was on vacation at the time of "The Great Ice Storm", and I know I was not as upset as the people who lost family members to the cold or who had their businesses looted. It felt very silly to be able to look at the giant nuclear reactor down the road, unable to provide us with power because the government-owned sticks and wires had fallen down.

None of this is even considering any potentially hidden sources of efficient energy that we do not have access to. There are many interesting devices available to provide us with alternative energy, yet these seem to be some of the most suppressed technologies around. Who does the suppressing? You can guess.

The last part of this centralized "public" utility thing that I have a problem with is the fact that tax dollars pay for the majority of the requisite infrastructure, but private companies are often or usually handed the ability to profit off of this afterward.

Public funds are used to build most of the system, yet private companies are given practically free reign to control it afterward. This usually means that prices are determined by these companies, who too often continually raise the price for these utilities.

This happens with roads sometimes too. In Ontario, the government spent 1.5 billion Canadian dollars building a highway (the 407), which they sold to a private operator for 3.1 billion. Taxpayers never once got to use this road without paying an extra toll. Taxpayers also never saw a penny from the 1.6 billion dollar profit. Of course the government said they would prevent this new private owner from increasing the toll "too much," and of course the government failed this task and the prices are now much higher than ever predicted.

In order to build highway 407, the government forced many property owners to "sell" the government their land. One of my friends had a manufacturing center for their business in this territory, and they were obliged to accept the "book price", or "market value" for their property. Market value did not account for the cost of building their workshop in the first place, let alone the cost of relocation.

When governments choose to build a highway, an airport, or a power station, they regularly steal land from citizens. It does not matter if their families have owned that land for generations. It does not matter if it will cost them more to move than is represented in the market price. Governments do not care for such trivial matters.[iii]

In a normal free market situation, *competition* between companies provides the incentive to offer *competitive prices*. Companies can't just charge whatever they want, because another company can offer their services at a better rate. When utilities come from massive centralized projects, funded by taxes, it is unrealistic to expect private companies to be able to compete – they can't afford to build infrastructure to compete with government funding. In any case, private companies are not allowed to build their own grid to compete.

This setup of public-gone-private has caused utility prices in many less-industrialized (poorer) countries to become unaffordable luxuries. Part of the justification for these things being "public" in the first place is so they can be available to the public at a reasonable rate. In our "modern" countries, most of us just have to put up with the steadily inflating costs, whether the utility is controlled by the government or a private company.

I am not against private businesses. But I am very against this buddy system between governments and giant corporations. This is not free market capitalism, this is tax-funded cronyism. The end result is expensive and inefficient utilities that end up completely out of the hands of the people who paid for them.

Water:

The main other type of infrastructure typically used in justifying government involvement is water. It is said that water systems for large populations are so big and important that we need a government to handle this.[iv]

I would actually make the same argument against this as I

would for centralized energy production and distribution. It is said that these "massive" projects require massive capital and maintenance, hence the need for government.

Governments are not the only entities capable of overseeing large-scale infrastructure projects. But this takes for granted the idea that these projects must be *centralized*. Public water and electric systems are large *because* they are centralized. But neither water nor electricity requires centralization.

Centralized water is a terrible thing, in my opinion. Maybe the Romans did it better with aquifers, but so far in the modern age we can only provide somewhat clean water that is expensive to distribute and is still laden with chemicals at the tap.

Whether the water is fluoridated or not, it will have industrial chemicals added in the name of safety. I do not know of any public water system anywhere in the world that does not at least use chlorine. Regardless of whether the small amount of chlorine is measurably harmful or not, many people, including myself, are uncomfortable with such sterilization agents in our drinking water.

Even with massive filters *and* chemicals, public water across the world is still full of unwanted material. From particulate matter to synthetic hormones to pharmaceutical drug residue, the product we pay for from the tap is, to put it mildly, unappetizing. In the health business, it is very easy to sell water filters simply by showing people what is in their tap water.

I don't think we can effectively or efficiently provide clean water to any modern human population through centralized pipes. I have yet to see an engineering plan that would allow this. Fortunately, water is easy to filter *closer to the point of use*. This is *decentralized* water.

Governments all over the world have taken a very strange stance on decentralized water. In most residential areas in modern countries, it is illegal for you to collect your own water from rain or river or air. Sometimes politicians will say that this is actually *for* our health – rain water is bad for us they say. Or, if we let everyone collect river water, there may be no water left downstream. "It's only fair."

These arguments fall apart once we realize how readily these same governments give permission to corporations to divert or dam entire rivers or lakes for commercial purposes. Logic is strained even further when we realize that perfectly clean water can be pulled directly from the air anywhere on Earth.

Most often, all of this is simply not talked about.

Part of the solution to the many problems of centralized public water is: decentralized, private water. Every house, building, farm, or homestead can and should filter its own water. The cost is carried by property owners. The pipes to carry this water from the filter to the tap are much shorter than the vast network of pipes and pumps required for public water.

For whole areas water can be pulled from the ground or the air, or desalinated from the oceans. Perhaps property taxes pay for the company to maintain the system. Some towns such as Kirkland Lake have it easier, using a neighboring lake as its primary water source, and wells, springs, and rivers for people outside of town. Any towns or cities that choose to use current water recycling systems should still filter every building, as that water will remain low quality.

This is possible in every city, town, and country dwelling on Earth. It is more cost efficient and safe to filter water on an as-needed basis, close to the point of use, than to filter water for a whole city and claim that it is clean – it might be sterile, but it is certainly not "clean". Those of us who are concerned about this already have to invest in water filters, because public water everywhere in the world is demonstrably unclean.

What about waste water? Like roads, the diversion and treatment of waste water is an engineering task that has nothing to do with bureaucrats. It wouldn't matter if we had a government or not, we'd have to figure out what to do with our waste, and a private company would likely be the ones dealing with it regardless.

These tasks can seem so large that it is natural to assume it also requires a large government to properly handle it. But governments have screwed up waste water in a long list of ways through history. From simply dumping it into a nearby water body untreated, to signing off on expensive systems that never worked, the government is not a reliable manager of complicated engineering.

Sometimes they do more than a bad job. In 2021 the Wisconsin Senate approved 'water cremation' for human bodies in Senate Bill 228. Water, heat, pressure, and lye are used to dissolve the human body. The pulverized bone material is returned to the family and the rest is washed into the municipal waste water system. This last part is what some people have a problem with.

Much of the systems we currently have in cities throughout the modern world are getting quite old and were never designed to handle extreme population densities. This is the reason why practically every city I have visited anywhere in the world, frankly, smells.

The modern world hasn't figured out waste water for the amount of people we are dealing with in today's cities. Paris is beautiful, and it smells terrible.[v] New York and Los Angeles can't be smelled in the movies. Stand near the Sydney Opera House to take the obligatory tourist photo, and you will smell our existing problem with waste water.

The current building trend in North America is either for more high rises in the dense city centers, and flatter sprawling development in suburban townships surrounding the cities. The cities will likely continue to experience major difficulties in their water, transportation infrastructure, wiring, and increased cost of maintenance as cost of living increases.

The newer suburbs of the sprawl will have an easier time building new and maintaining old infrastructure. The rural environment will remain as it is, with plenty of options for drinking water, waste disposal, and energy production.

Though I am not in favor of "progressive" taxes (higher taxes for those who earn more money), when it comes to roads and other civic infrastructure, I am in favor of money being spent close to home. Cities cost more than towns; they have expensive things like subway systems, large industrial capacities, mega highways, and likely also public parks and walkways that are reasonably maintained. But they also bring in a lot more revenue. The money to pay for roads and electricity and schools should already be there. Property taxes don't exist everywhere, but it wouldn't require a formal government, at least not a federal or state government, to oversee expenditures of property taxes for local infrastructure. Or the money could come from somewhere else – but it will have to come from somewhere.

If the property tax rate were set by the local government, based on what the budget actually requires, people could choose to live in more or less expensive places – the tax itself might be mandatory in each proper municipality, but you could choose to live in a town or city with a lower rate. However it is paid for, the road workers would still be private companies as they are today, the water can continue to be mostly run privately, and we can open the doors to the possibilities of mixed energy production, both on and off grid.

All laws must be enforceable. If a tax is mandatory, a threat is implicitly included that there will be punishment for detractors. We will discuss police in later chapters, but for now I will say that rules can still exist in absence of law, as long as the people are "allowed" to enforce them. Someone would have to penalize the detractors if a property tax were mandatory. I am more in favor of a voluntary system. I might even be proud to pay a voluntary tax that satisfied our infrastructure demands efficiently. There is more to say on this but there is also more to consider before we get there.

3. Food.

You could be forgiven for thinking that the government doesn't have that much to do with food. We tend to think of food as a private enterprise thing, or maybe a United Nations World Food Programme thing.

Modern governments have an awful lot to do with our food, at the highest level of production down to the lowest level of distribution. If you read a history of governments, it is likely that the story will start all the way back at the dawn of the "agricultural age." Our supposed shift from "hunting and gathering" to farming is a large part of the justifications for kingdoms and eventually governments to exist in the first place.

Sometimes this story is painted in a rather egalitarian way. It is said that the centralization of food production required administration for efficient and fair distribution, and protection of settlements from raiders. This administration became what we now know as the government.

I don't know if food distribution was ever a necessary administrative need, but that is the story. The problem with the story is that it seems to have nothing at all to do with actually getting food to people who are outside of the government.

Early governments came up with "taxes." Regular people made or collected or grew things, and the government had the idea of taking some of it forcibly, largely to pay or feed the armed men who worked for the government. The products in question were often salt and grains. The word "salary" comes from this original salt payment, and salt tax.

You might think that the people who made or collected or grew things could have simply made them available to the people themselves. Early monetary systems seem usually to have been based on credit. Such natural credit arrangements still exist today in places where governments do not operate, and in any case people everywhere have always been capable of bringing their goods directly to the market.

The farmers grew things that they could have sold for cash, which has existed on and off for all of recorded human history – with and without a centralized, government-based monetary system. More likely, they would have "traded" their goods and services based on a credit system. They even could have bartered, if they were feeling primitive. I doubt any farmer would have come up with the idea to voluntarily give a portion of it to the king, in return for nothing other than the vague mafia-style "protection."

Taxes were collected in order to feed the armed forces of the king. Law itself is founded on the idea of protecting "the king's peace." These armed forces historically are also the people doing the collecting of the stuff from the citizens. Suddenly the picture doesn't seem so egalitarian, but this is history.

Since then, nothing has really changed. Laws still exist to protect and empower the government, and taxes are still collected to facilitate this. Only now we have much more complicated collection and distribution systems for this forced taxation.

From the earliest records of government, we have them interfering with the food system. At some point in time the government decided to support certain foods and other material production, such as weapons.

"Support" sounds like a nice thing, but this "support" comes mainly in the form of giving tax incentives to farmers and other producers who themselves also have to forcibly pay their own taxes. Seems kind of circular and wasteful.

The word "subsidy" is one of the most insidious words in the English language. It is now commonly used to reference government "support", but the original meaning is either "to hire mercenaries," or "to bribe." Bet you don't think of that when the television news talks of government subsidies, but that is exactly what a subsidy is – forcibly collected tax dollars by hired mercenaries, redistributed in the form of a bribe.

The two favorite types of products our governments subsidize are weapons and food. These two products don't seem to be related, but they are – you control a population with weapons and food.

The US government currently subsidizes 9 main foods, and it is worth going through each one.

Corn:

Corn is used mainly as a type of sugar – high fructose corn syrup. I have a hard time calling this product "food." I enjoy a corn on the cob as much as the next guy, but this corn syrup is the backbone of the modern junk food industry.

Corn is also used to make ethanol, which they call "biofuel." Biofuel is promoted as a way to "combat global warming," which we will get into further in later chapters.

Something to note about biofuel is that it is less efficient than conventional petrol-based fuels. Biofuels are also harder on conventional motors and pipes, producing more wear and less overall vehicle efficiency over its lifetime. Biofuels also require massive amounts of conventional petroleum products in order to grow the corn, process it, and transport it. It also requires massive amounts of water. To top it off, corn ethanol is corrosive to conventional pipelines, making transportation of this fuel an additional expense and challenge.

The US government, as well as several other governments, have forced fuel retailers to include this subsidized, inefficient, motor-ruining biofuel in their mixtures. Much of this growing is done in foreign countries, and much of this newly cleared land was, and is high-biodiversity forest such as the Amazon.

By the way, the exhaust from corn fuel is practically the same as from regular gasoline.

The government says oil is bad, so they bribe farmers around the world to grow corn. Most farmland is already being used for something, so new farmland tends to need to be "cleared." The same people who are supporting the use of biofuels to "save the Earth," are also actively supporting the clearing of pristine, old-growth forests.

This newly cleared land is poor quality farmland. Forest soils can support a forest, but they hardly support farming. The best farmlands are those that are easily replenished with yearly flooding of mineral rich water. Since most forests do not exist in this environment, this newly cleared forest farmland quickly turns to dust, forcing the bribed farmers to clear more land to grow new corn crops.

Since this crop is "subsidized," this corn is now available to the market at less than its inherent value – the value that would traditionally be determined as a result of the cost of production and distribution, and market demand.

Since this product is now cheaper than it would naturally be on a free market, junk food producers are able to use this ingredient to make cheap junk food.

To believe that biofuels are a good idea, we first have to accept that conventional petroleum is finite. Scarcity is easy to invent. It is worth mentioning that there are many people, including myself, who do not believe that oil is finite or derived from "fossils," but to fully substantiate that belief would require another book. For now, it is widely accepted that biofuels are far less efficient than conventional fuels, and the supposed date for "peak oil" production keeps getting pushed further into the future.

I do not believe that corn should be subsidized. Real businesses do not require subsidies. Real businesses can produce a product and sell it to the market at the price determined by the market. This system works fine for foods that are not subsidized. Governments seem to have special interest in supporting the junk food industry and the logically-backwards biofuel industry.

Wheat:

The wheat of today is not the same as the wheat of ancient times. The compounds that modern dieters have problems with in grains were less abundant in the "ancient grains." Pre-modern recipes that used flours typically had other fortifying factors, such as bone meal, fine wood ash, spices, fruits, and more. Today's wheat products are mostly based on processed flour and processed sugar. In the recommended reading section at the end of the book I have cited some excellent resources on this subject, and the effect these ingredients had on our health.

Even if we were eating the same wheat that Jesus did, I would still not agree with subsidizing this food. Those of us who believe in free markets, believe that everything can be produced at a fair price based on supply and demand.

Governments seem not to believe in supply and demand. They seem to believe that forcibly manipulating supply will coerce changes in demand. They seem to believe that products which have had an existing place in the market for all of human history suddenly need a helpful bribe, paid for by us, the taxpayers.

At this point it is worth saying that there is no such thing as "government money." The government does not make money. They might print money – though this is typically done by private businesses such as the US Federal Reserve – but they do not produce any actual value.

I would prefer if governments operated like a business. Businesses have to supply some value in order to be rewarded by the market. My point here is that we can sometimes think that this is "government money" paying for these silly things like biofuels. In reality, it is our money. The government does not profit – we profit, and the government takes some of our profits.

They use some of our money to bribe wheat farmers. Like corn, wheat flour is core to the non-foods we call "junk." Take away corn and wheat subsidies, and junk food would not be as easily affordable. I think this would be a great thing.

Soy:

There is a similar case to be made for soy as with corn and wheat. This is an ancient food that people have always been willing to buy at market value. Governments justify their involvement with some of these products by "maintaining prices" on these core foods to "help low-income farmers, and aid rural development."

Similar to wheat and corn, modern soy is both chemically different from its ancient counterpart, and it is used as a highly processed ingredient in modern junk food. The government once again in effect is taking our money and using it to make junk food cheaper.

Together these three foods – corn, wheat, and soy – comprise a large portion of the calories fed to our livestock animals. Describing the proper diets of cows, pigs, and chickens is beyond the scope of this book, but we should all know that our livestock species are not optimally nourished on these foods, and these ingredients are used largely as "filler," with nutrients added in for actual nourishment. We feed our livestock these "junk" ingredients, and we are left with lower quality animal products, hence the rise of interest in "grass fed" and "free range" animal products.

Rice:

Rice is subsidized by governments, and for the life of me I cannot understand why. Rice is hardly grown in the western world – it is largely grown in the same Asian countries as it always has been. Why do our governments subsidize rice? I have no idea.

Rice is not a staple or necessary food in our western cultures. It is also quite cheap already, without subsidies. This crop is known as a peasant food, partially because peasants have always been able to afford it. Why are we paying for peasant food? I simply don't know.

Beer:

Believe it or not, beer is subsidized in America. Why? Excellent question.

Beer is fermented grains, usually wheat, barley, or rye. Sometimes rice. Rice-based beers have less problematic proteins, and so they are much less harmful than beers based on the gluten grains of wheat, barley, and rye.

At one point the American government banned beer and other alcohols. I don't like the idea of government banning anything, but at least reduced alcohol consumption is good for us. Now they take our money and use it to make beer cheaper, and I have no idea why.

I asked the internet why the government subsidizes beer, and the only answer I can find is essentially that the alcohol industry has a strong relationship with the government. Ask, and ye shall receive.

Milk & Beef:

Milk and beef are both subsidized by the American government. The situation is similar in many countries. I do not believe that dairy farmers need to be bribed in order to remain in business. In 2020, the United States Department of Agriculture reported that dairy products are at record high consumption in America. Demand has continually increased for five straight decades. Despite some ups and downs in the beef and other meat industries, demand has continued to increase since records have been taken.

Some countries tax foods that they want to limit the consumption of, but not all countries subsidize foods that have perfectly healthy demand and industrial infrastructure.

Peanut Butter:

Peanuts are a cheap food that is more resistant to climate events than many other crops. Peanuts are beans that grow easily and can be stored and transported easily. Peanut butter is made cheaper because of government subsidies, and again the only reason I can find for this is strong relationships with the peanut industry and the government.

I am in the "alternative health" business in real life. If you asked me to choose one "nut" to subsidize, it would not be the peanut. Peanuts are actually legumes, and as a legume they are incredibly easy to produce and process, and have less nutritional value than actual nuts. I would probably pick the almond to support, as we like to call the almond the "king of the nuts."

Really, I would not support any food subsidy. The peanut and the almond have their own inherent value and an easily determined market value based on supply and demand.

Sunflower Oil:

Sunflower oil is a cheap, inflammatory oil used in fast foods and junk foods. Inflammation is not good.

Oils are present in every tissue in nature. The oil in a seed, or a nut, or a leaf, or any food, is protected from "oxidation" by the living skin, peel, or shell of the plant or animal.

Oxidation is a natural process that happens when energy is used. We produce "free" oxygen molecules known as "free radicals" when we exercise and when we eat. Oxygen is highly reactive, and so these free radicals cause chemical damage when they attempt to bond with other particles in our bodies.

The textbook explanation of this is more complicated, but this is the gist of it. Free radicals are natural, but too many of them are bad. We must use nutrients known as "anti-oxidants" to mitigate this process in the body. We will still gradually accumulate damage just by being alive, breathing and eating, and this accounts for much of what we call "aging."

All oils oxidize. Some fats and oils are much more resistant to oxidation. They can last for longer in the open air, and they can take more heat before being converted into free radicals. Sunflower oil is not one of these strong oils. Sunflower oil is practically all free radicals, especially if it is processed with heat.

Since sunflower oil is almost always used in cheap junk and fast foods, you can usually guarantee that high heat is used in the production. This is bad. Oxidation contributes to all degenerative diseases, clogged arteries, and cancers. The government is paying for one of the worst ingredients we could be using in any food.

None of these foods require government intervention. Most of these foods are outright harmful in our modern food system. These foods together comprise the majority of calories consumed by Americans, and I do not think this is a coincidence – cheaper foods are more readily consumed.

Government involvement with food is unequivocally bad for us. It has made bad foods more available to people who do not need them.

Governments also try to give us advice on what to eat, and we will see in the next chapter that this is also a bad situation.

4. Health.

I firmly believe that government involvement with healthcare is the worst possible thing ever to have happened to human health.

We saw in the food chapter that the government takes some of our money and supports junk foods and alcohols. Overconsumption of foods in general, and bad foods in particular, is one of the biggest health problems in the modern world.

From my perspective in the "alternative" health business, most people's biggest problem is that they eat too much food, and usually the wrong foods. Decreasing food alone will improve most people's health dramatically and quickly. Entirely eliminating at least 4 of the foods on the subsidized list (corn, wheat, soy, and beer), will outright *eliminate most common health problems.*

In the chapter on research and development I will speak more about government waste for useless research, but when it comes to food I really wish I had a better idea of what goes on inside government laboratories.

Somehow the main governments of the world have come up with food recommendations that are essentially the opposite of what we advise our customers to do if they want to get healthier.

To say this another way, if you ate exactly the opposite of

how the government recommends, you will probably become noticeably healthier quite quickly.

It almost seems like a conspiracy. I don't know how they got things so wrong without doing this deliberately. I say this because we have very adequately mapped the nutritional requirements and formulas for animal nutrition, paid for largely by the government. Every animal industry utilizes this information to maintain healthy stocks of animals. At least one department understands nutrition – just not one that deals with human health.

I am from a country with "free" healthcare. Like the phrase "government money," this "free" concept is very misleading. Nothing is free. We pay *for* government. Anything the government does is a product of our money. Give me your money and I will give you a free slap in the face, basically.

Let's get this out of the way: your health is *your* responsibility, not the government's. You control what food, supplements, and substances go into or do not go into your mouth. Your decisions about these products will determine your health. If you make the wrong choices, you will develop a health problem.

The absolute best that a doctor can do for you – no matter who pays for the doctor – is try to deal with your mistakes. This is a terrible system. This is akin to never changing the oil in your vehicle until the engine seizes – every time.

If mechanics were paid by government insurance, they would probably never tell you about oil changes. Don't worry, insurance pays. Eat whatever you want, come see us when something breaks.

In our business of alternative health, we teach people to be in control of what goes into their bodies. This is the largest factor in their overall health. If they do this correctly, they should hardly need to see us or any medical professionals.

Emergency care *is* available for accidents and infections, but this is not the primary use of the existing medical system. If hospitals only had to deal with accidents and infections, hospitals would be much smaller and slower, and much of the medical industry would be out of work.

This is not just true in countries with government health insurance. All countries that rely on the allopathic (mainstream) medical system have a standard of putting out fires instead of preventing them – "treating" health problems, instead of preventing them. When insurance pays for this, we seem not to care. We're the ones who have to pay for prevention.

This wouldn't be such a big deal if the human body worked the way mainstream medicine believes. If drugs, tests, and surgeries actually fixed health problems, we wouldn't have much of a business selling preventative health strategies. The abhorrent failure of modern medicine is the reason we are in a growing market for "alternative" strategies.

The government never had anything to do with our health. The government does not subsidize healthy foods or nutrition, but even if they did, I would argue that the market is capable of producing great foods and supplements, and us consumers are completely capable of paying for it.

The system of preventative healthcare is used in all animal industries. Farmers, pet breeders, and zoo keepers systematically prevent and reverse diseases and birth defects with simple nutritional strategies. Emergency care and medicines are rarely required, and generally if your animals have a health problem it is your fault.

We don't typically have health insurance for animals and this is the reason the market has come up with economical nutritional solutions to health problems.

Government insurance does not do anything for our health. There is no insurance program that will prevent disease.

The largest contributing factor for the recent decrease in the diseases that plagued our industrial societies, is hygiene. Tax money might have built many water systems, but we still now know the key to keeping many of the most serious diseases away: soap and water.

Most people haven't heard any of this because of the allopathic monopoly on healthcare. Allopathic medicine does not educate their practitioners in nutrition or prevention. They are there to deal with things once they break, and they do not have much or any incentive to help you prevent the diseases they are paid to treat, even if they knew how to prevent them. The allopathic professions in general have a terrible track record when it comes to actually fixing diseases, and their treatments include risks of side effects and death. I go into much more detail about this in my book *Fake Diseases*, but for the purposes of this book it is worth mentioning that this ignorant monopoly is fiercely supported by the government.

Worse, censorship of alternative views can be enforced by law. If you were to sit down with me and pay me for my alternative advice, I am supposed to ask you to sign a waiver that says something like: "this guy is a quack and his advice is questionable."

When I give a presentation I am supposed to say: "this information has not been evaluated by the FDA (or Health Canada), is not intended to diagnose, treat, or cure anything, and you should still see a licensed professional." Guess who gets to be licensed? Only professionals deemed worthy by the protected medical monopoly are allowed to be licensed medical practitioners.

I once gave a talk in Tijuana, Mexico. I was giving my normal disclaimer that "this information is not intended to diagnose, treat, or cure any disease.." when my host politely interjected. "My friend.." he said, "..here in Mexico, you can speak freely." What a concept! No wonder "medical tourism" is so popular in countries with less government "oversight" – customers can ask direct questions, and actually get direct answers in plain language that we all understand.

In America and Canada, a big part of our training has nothing to do with the actual protocols we recommend to people – we spend as much, or *more* time learning how to speak legally about health problems.[vi]

This is not a free market situation. Most people have no idea how many treatment options are available on the medical marketplace. They don't know this because the government supports the most incompetent medical group and officially denounces the rest.

Government involvement with healthcare covers both of my basic grievances with governments. They fail to support our health, largely because our health is, was, and always will be *our business*, not anyone else's. And they *harm us* with their support of a medical system that does a terrible job outside of trauma care and a handful of infectious diseases.

In many modern countries I can actually be criminally charged for "treating" you by unconventional means. Legally, if you want to deal with me, we have to avoid the words "treat" or "cure" in reference to a specific disease or symptom. How is this supposed to help you? It isn't – this system is in place to protect the allopathic medical monopoly.

Theoretically, the government could ban unhealthy foods and force us to take supplements, but I would say that this is bad. I believe in freedom more than I believe in good health. That sounds backwards coming from someone in the health business, but quality of life is most important to me, and I would not appreciate being forced to do anything.

For the government to enforce good health we would have to believe that the government *knows* how to support health. Every government has different general health recommendations, and none of them are what I would say is optimal. There is not much agreement among practitioners of different schools of thought around how to best achieve good health and healing.

I believe that we consumers should be the ultimate decision makers when it comes to which advice to apply to our bodies. This system only works if we have free access to all of the available information, and ingredients. Our governments ensure that we do not have this open access.

If we knew exactly what to do to produce reliable health effects, there might be some argument to be made about government responsibility to ensure this. Either way, this would eradicate your freedom to choose what goes into your body.

In our camp, we might argue that we have a good understanding of what would need to be done to ensure reliable, predictable good health. If you asked us how to accomplish this, our program would be similar to cattle feed. Livestock feeds are standardized to ensure that basic nutrition covers all their general needs. This produces reliable stocks of healthy calves each year, and predictable growth rates and lifespans.

This works great for livestock. But we are not livestock. Cows and pigs and sheep and chickens do very well under standardized systems, but they live in a prison. They are fed what and when we say, with no accounting for taste or enjoyment. They live in controlled conditions from birth until death, and both of those processes are also overseen by the master humans.

This is hardly desirable for human life, yet that is what proper government control over our health would look like. An even worse scenario can be imagined where *incorrect* health protocols are forced. Since governments across the world currently provide terrible advice on basic health strategies, we would expect terrible results if they were able to enforce their own guidelines.

An excellent case study is water fluoridation.

Fluoride is a naturally occurring element found in spring water and other sources all over the world. If you ask us, we will say that all natural elements are probably essential for optimal human health and longevity. But each element can harm or kill us in the wrong form or dose.

Arsenic is an agreed essential mineral for all vertebrates. All creatures with a spine require a small amount of arsenic, or they develop a disease and die prematurely. This is not controversial. All animal feeds include arsenic. Obviously, the incorrect dose of arsenic is a big problem – it can kill us.

Fluoride is similar. Governments seem to believe that naturally occurring fluoride is the same as chemical fluoride produced as a byproduct of industrial manufacturing. Another word for "byproduct" is "waste." Chemical fluoride is industrial waste.

When a chemical agent is given to a person for a medical purpose, this agent is called a "medicine," or a "drug." In the western world, a licensed practitioner known as a "doctor" is the only professional able to legally "prescribe" a medicine.

A prescription is supposed to result only from what is known as "informed consent." The consumer is meant to be educated by the doctor about the potential risks and rewards of the treatment being proposed, and then decide whether to accept the prescription.

This is a voluntary situation. The patient can choose to take the doctor's recommendation, or not. This is good – it allows us to control what goes into our body.

Doctors and medical science are not perfect, and so the law does not allow them to act without consent of the patient except in limited circumstances such as you showing up to the hospital unconscious.

One of the many reasons this concept of controlled prescriptions is good is because appropriate doses of medications (and nutrients) are based on many variables. A person's state of health, their body weight, and whether or not they are pregnant or nursing are a few of the more important variables to consider when deciding which doses of chemical agents we should use for treatment of health problems.

A dose of a medicine only makes sense in the context of the body it is being put into. A 200 pound adult and a 20 pound child require very different doses. The same dose will be ten times stronger in the child than the adult. When a drug is put into the drinking water, the doses are not controlled. The child and the adult and the old lady and the cancer patient are all being given the same absolute dose, but the *relative* dose will be different for each of them.

There is no drug in existence where it would be appropriate to dose in this random fashion, yet this is what the government has done in the case of fluoride.

I have a very hard time believing that my government cares about my teeth – especially since we pay for our own dental care. I have an even harder time believing that an industrial byproduct with a skull and crossbones label on it is an appropriate treatment for "tooth decay" – especially when my teeth are fine and I am in the business of helping people achieve perfect dental health through nutrition.

Further, I belong to a large and growing group of people who believe that the chemical drug called fluoride in our drinking water is actively *harmful*. Because of this belief, and because of the other things in the water, I choose to filter my drinking and cooking water. We would also recommend filtering shower water, as these chemicals are readily absorbed through the skin and eyes.

I don't believe that this was a simple botch. I believe this chemical was costing an industry a lot of money to dispose of, and friends in the government allowed them to offset these costs by adding it into the public water system. It was a brilliant scam, because the government ended up paying industry for this waste, rather than industry having to pay for waste disposal. This history is well documented, so it is not a conspiracy theory – it *is* a conspiracy, but it is not a theory.

In the best case of this debacle, the government overstepped its right to interfere with our health and made a terrible mistake, prescribing everyone a harmful drug without their consent. In the worst case, the government knowingly introduced a toxic agent, at our expense of both tax money and our health.

With this precedent of government acting on our behalf without our informed consent, there is really nothing stopping them from expanding this program to include other drugs forced into our bodies at our expense. This is bad for both our freedom and our health.

I do not personally care whether fluoride, or vaccines, or birth control, or any other drugs have a positive or negative net benefit to my health or the health of the population in general. I care about our right to decide what goes into our bodies.

The government provides expensive water that I feel is un-drinkable. It has also inched its way towards controlling how we are medicated. This is a disaster. It is even worse that we have to pay for this.

There is no scenario in which it would be smart of us to leave our health in the hands of any government.

In 2020 governments around the world decided to imple-ment the largest-scale public health protocol ever imag-ined, in response to a virus. I believe this was a deliberate conspiracy to further increase government power and de-crease civilian power, but even if this were truly a humani-tarian action, I believe the consequences of the forced busi-ness closures and mass house arrests were worse than the sickness. The cure should not be worse than the disease.

In Ontario, there has at the time of writing been reported over two million workers affected, and over two hundred thousand businesses closed. No virus caused these clo-sures, this was a direct consequence of a government pro-gram.

I once spent a year in Windsor, Ontario, near the southern tip of the country and conveniently just a bridge or tunnel trip away from Detroit, Michigan. At the time and until the closures, the small city was doing quite well. It is isolated from the major population centers and has its own culture and spirit, and with its status as a border town it has multi-ple businesses dependent on cross border travel. But the governments closed the borders in March 2020, and at the time of writing, over 16 months later, they are still closed.

I had to go through Windsor recently and I could hardly be-lieve how much of the city was boarded up, clearly closed for good, and how many homeless people were absolutely everywhere. It is quite difficult to quantify exactly how hard hit an area has been from the pandemic closures, but in Windsor it is not hard to tell. Later I searched the internet for some statistics, and there were many articles about Windsor being one of the hardest hit cities in Canada.

Back when I first moved to Windsor, my mother dropped me off that day. The house I was staying in was on a wide boulevard with big old trees lining and shading the street. The people were friendly to me, and our small business did reasonably well. I made many friends and until 2020 I considered it one of the best towns to live in in the province. When I drove through it this time, the state of the place brought a few tears to my eyes.

Niagara Falls, Ontario, is another border town heavily dependent on traffic and tourism. Its entertainment strip and city core were of course ghost towns when I went through there. The streets weren't empty in Niagara because of a virus. The closures were an effect of government. I bring this up in the health chapter, rather than the business chapter, because even though this is an economic problem, it was carried out in the name of health – for our own good.

Many people have commented on the potential for increased suicides and spousal abuse, among other potential problems, as a consequence of forced house arrest for hundreds of millions of people across the world. I do believe that the personal and social consequences of the Draconian government shutdowns are far worse than the virus.

The Johns Hopkins Psychiatry Guide states that the government-created pandemic mandates have exasperated multiple factors that may increase suicides. Economic stress is strongly correlated with suicide, as is social isolation. Participation in religious communities is associated with lower suicide rates, which was nullified when governments forced all church activities to cease.

Further, they state, "continuous media coverage of the pandemic may intensify anxiety and fear for individuals with preexisting mental health conditions." I strongly agree.

Further still, "barriers to mental health treatment that have arisen due to the pandemic include increased restrictions at healthcare facilities." The government created a scenario which is highly stressful, and simultaneously cut us off from access to mental healthcare. For our own good, of course.

Most people who have run the numbers say that suicide rates have not risen as dramatically as is being widely claimed, though they all recognize a difficulty in parsing the statistics. They all acknowledge, however, the great stress that has been put onto us by the government closures, and I would call all of this stress unnecessary.

One thing we alternative people near unanimously agree on, along with the mainstream medical world, is that stress is one of the most important factors for all disease.

One of the responses to this health crisis was for governments all over the world to force their citizens to wear face coverings. In some cases, like when performing surgery, wearing a covering is quite a good idea. But for healthy people, I believe the coverings are harmful, and does nothing to reduce the spread of a virus.

One of the simple but underrated things we promote in the alternative health world is *breathing*. I am a huge believer in deep breathing, multiple times daily, and strong breathing throughout the day. The lungs do more than intake oxygen, they also expel waste. One major problem that already existed before covering mandates was the lack of full deep breathing, completely expelling the old waste air at the bottom of the lungs, replaced regularly with fresh air. Now we have a new problem, with that waste material being partially trapped in the covering.

I have only had to wear one in airports and airplanes, and I can definitely say that I miss the deep breaths as soon as they are prevented. The way to breathe in a mask is more shallow and rapid – the exact opposite of what we would recommend for good health. In some places this mandate seems permanent, and I can only predict that this will measurably impact the health of anyone who has to regularly restrict their breathing.

One of the strangest government decisions during this pandemic was to shut down public rest stops on the roads and lock up the toilets at these locations. This wasn't done everywhere, but it was done in Ontario. Given that good hygiene is probably the largest factor in the modern eradication of infectious disease, it baffles me that anyone claiming to make a decision *for public health* would eliminate public bathrooms – *more* opportunities to wash hands should make sense.

This decision made the roads less safe, by reducing the ability to rest on highway trips, and the spread of germs more likely, by reducing soap and water availability. Worse, we still had to pay the exact same budget during this period, with no discount for the long list of removed services.

I will say a bit more on this in the business chapter, but for now it is my opinion that this unprecedented social, economic, and medical disaster is purely the fault of governments apparently acting "for our own good."

Every bit of power we give the government over our health is bad for us. The only way the government could possibly help our health is by forcing the equivalent of cattle feed into us, and offering us absolutely no control over what goes into our body.

We do not need government middlemen to oversee hospitals for trauma or emergency care. This can be fully facilitated by private businesses. Government involvement merely produces the opportunity for the medical system to milk us for insurance money.

Under government insurance, doctors and hospitals are incentivized to over-prescribe, over-treat, bill for things that aren't necessary, or bill for things that never happened. This system offers no incentive for doctors or hospitals, or any healthcare professional to offer you any advice or treatment aimed at prevention.

Preventing health problems is much cheaper and easier than attempting to fix them later. Governments logically would want to encourage prevention, especially if they pay for the healthcare. Unfortunately, governments do not operate on logic, and instead of a focus on prevention there is only a focus on dangerous and expensive treatments.

5. Environment.

Now things get a bit more complicated. I do believe that government policies around the world have made it harder for the people and the business world to rectify environmental wrongs, but there is an elephant in the room that might seem to conflict with the title of this book.

One supposedly good thing governments have done is to create protected zones of land and ocean, known as national parks or environmental protection zones. Am I really going to make the case that these are bad things? Yes.

To start with, I have the same basic problem with the phrase "public property" as I do with "government money." It is a mislabeling. "Public" property is not in any realistic way owned or controlled by the public. Public property is government property, with rules enforced by government agents.

In Canada and other "commonwealth" countries, public land that is not part of a national park is called "crown land." This implies that it belongs to the Queen of England. We do apparently have a right to use this land in emergency situations – for example, we are allowed to use natural resources to build ourselves a temporary shelter, if needed.

Beyond that, we are extremely limited in the use of this land. We can purchase a hunting license from the government – some would call this a "hunting tax" – and we can pay for the right to shoot or trap a certain animal. For this we are issued a "tag" for that animal. I am not going to spend much time griping about hunting taxes, my point here is only that this is hardly "public" land – the few activities we are allowed to use this land for, we usually have to pay additional fees for.

One might argue that this restriction on the use of land is good for the environment, and if it is good for the environment then it is automatically good for us. They might also argue that this government involvement prevents commercial exploitation of natural resources.

To the first point, I would beg to differ. There is a balance that even the most strident environmentalists believe in – it is not purely and unanimously good to have the environment trump human needs. Life on earth would be terrible for humans if we could not cut a single tree or kill a single wolf – including the one trying to eat us.

I value the environment. I like animals. Biodiversity is good. And there is a balance we can aim for between environmental interests and our own. Further, in modern times forested areas have expanded dramatically since the industrial revolution, and I think this is great. I am not willing to credit the government with this improvement. One reason we deforested much of the world was for wood to burn as fuel. Industry – private business – was responsible for the innovations that decreased our dependence on destructive practices.

Industry has continued to improve its practices, including cleaner mining and transport of oil – despite the few highly publicized mistakes like the Exxon Valdez spill in Alaska and the British Petroleum leak in the Gulf of Mexico. In general, humanity and industry is decreasing its footprint per industrial activity. Government has very little to do with this.

To the point about "protected" lands being safe from commercial exploitation, I would point out that lands only seem to be protected from civilian use. When there is strong commercial incentive to exploit something – to build a pipeline or mine a territory – there seems to be some way around the protection. This is cronyism once again, and it does happen all too often. Governments can and do violate their own protected areas in favor of industry.

There is a concept in the academic world used to prop up government involvement with the environment. It is called "the tragedy of the commons." It is said that, given unlimited access to limited resources, humans will basically deplete the resource through competition with each other to take the most.

I have always thought this argument was a "straw man" - an intentionally misrepresented proposition that is set up because it is easier to defeat than an opponent's real argument.

There is hardly any evidence that governments actually prevent over-exploitation. Yet the academic world still says things like "nothing short of the government with its power of regulating an industry for the common good can stop such an outbreak of cutthroat competition."

Anyone familiar with the commercial fishing industry will beg to differ. Most of the worst offenders are from fully modern industrialized countries in Europe, gleefully scraping the shallows of every ocean in the world – the equivalent of strip-mining for seafood. Regulations have done absolutely nothing to curtail the problem. The problem is worse now than it has ever been – the vessels are larger and the demand for seafood is greater than ever.

It is ignorance about how fish are caught that explains the lack of consumer demand for better practices. The solution, in my opinion, is to increase awareness about fishing practices, and the market will regulate itself through consumer demands and industry response.[vii]

There is indeed a tragedy of the commons, but the problem is not solved by government. Anyone who has ever walked through the halls of an old apartment building knows that the greasy stains and cigarette burns are the result of this tragedy of the commons. But the solution to a lack of care for public space is not simply to appoint government overseers to the property – the solution, in my opinion, is to promote greater stewardship through *ownership*.

For the optimal human incentive to care for the hallway, people should own their own hallways. This doesn't really work for oceans, but we do have the ability to communicate with industries, and it is already common that consumer money is being spent on more apparently Earth-friendly products.

I am not claiming here to know the solution to the many problems our oceans face, but I do not believe that government is the answer, and the whole narrative of "we need government to regulate everything" is something I do not agree with.

Apartment buildings are designed to extract maximum rent per dollar of investment by the builder or investor. They are not designed to facilitate optimal human experience. The problem with the "tragedy of the commons" in the hallways is not solved by government regulations, or government oversight. Since residents are not incentivized to clean the hallways, someone probably must be paid to do it.

Apartment buildings are also promoted by governments. Nearly all "public housing" takes the shape of an apartment building. This is again to maximize the efficiency of dollars invested, not to maximize human wellbeing. Maybe we should not aim to live in them. Nonetheless, governments all over the world seem very keen on attracting more and more people to densely concentrated living, invariably in buildings.

Most people would consider the words "sustainable development" to be a good thing. I once would have agreed, before I understood who introduced these terms and why. Sustainable development is part of "Agenda 21." This is the plan to completely control humanity, in the name of saving the Earth, by way of sustainable development. For a full explanation of what is known as Agenda 21, I recommend the book *Endgame* by Vernon Coleman.

National parks are part of Agenda 21. The people who control much of this world's resources seem to believe that the common people must be prevented from having any share of it. They say that to save the Earth we must live packed in dense cities with little access to and no rights over the natural environment. This sounds like a conspiracy theory but these are official United Nations goals.

Sustainable development is a packaged plan sold to us through guilt and fear. We can debate each individual reason given for the continual removal of rights of people and increasing power of government, but I will take the wide view and condemn the entire thing as a simple exercise of power in the aim of world domination by a world government.

If we do accept that the government must prevent people from "exploiting" anything, then we seem to be endorsing full-scale control over our lives. I do not see a middle ground when the government is empowered to make decisions about what is best for the whole world, including humanity and "the environment."

This is why national parks are bad for us – the laws in place to "protect the environment" inevitably remove rights from us. We get more taxes and fees and government employees, and this is not necessary for the thriving of either the environment or us.

This goes right back to the health chapter. Do we believe anyone should be empowered to make these massively important decisions on our behalf? I do not believe so.

I believe the people create something known as "the market," and the market can demand that companies act responsibly. This process is sometimes interfered with by government though buddy partnerships with industry. We seem hardly able to make any impact on the decisions of major businesses that operate under the arm of government protection.

In any case, better practices tend to take time to implement, and we have been improving over time. But governments give companies the right to build a pipeline or drain a lake to mine, and we seem unable to do anything about it. Worse, it is government mercenaries who show up to interfere with protests of such situations.

I believe that every environmental initiative supported by the government is much more about stripping rights and power from people. In many cases, such as the biofuel debacle, their policies do great harm to the environment. In others, we are restricted from doing certain things, while some groups of people or businesses are allowed to exploit them at will.

In Canada there is a group of people given free reign to kill any animal they please without any licenses or tags. I am against licenses, but I am also in favor of fairness.

"Native" Canadians have no restrictions on their hunting. We are told that this is "only fair," because "we" "took their lands." I do not feel that I took anyone's land. My family settled in Canada less than a hundred years ago, long after the initial invasion. I would say plainly: *the government took their land*. We are blamed for it, and we are meant to feel guilty and look the other way when these oppressed people kill "protected" species, yet we need a license *and* a tag to hunt non-protected species.

I have never hunted. I don't own a gun, and my firearms license is expired. I just don't like fake sympathy and forced favoritism. This group of people has been historically oppressed by our government since Europeans showed up here in history. Native "reserves" are still described as "third world" by pretty much anyone who has anything to say about them.

We need the government to protect the environment, except when it has some special agenda with an oppressed group or favored industry. Why can't we all operate under the same rules? Because the government says so.

Think about it for yourself for a moment. In what way does government involvement with "environmental protection" actually benefit us? I can't come up with an answer.

We are led to believe that we have nearly destroyed the entire environment, and this is a big part of why "something MUST be done." Drastic measures must be taken, or there will be nothing left for our children, we are told.

This party line only succeeds because the people are largely hearing this *inside* cities. Most of our populations have never even been a significant distance from the cities. If they had been around the huge country of Canada, they would know that there is absolutely no shortage of "nature." This is true in America as well, and Australia and many other countries where this "WE'RE DESTROYING EVERYTHING!" propaganda campaign is strongest.

Though there are many environmental problems, wildlife populations generally have improved since the industrial dawn, and today environmental consciousness has created millions of people who choose to support businesses that are attempting to be more environmentally friendly. This is great. I don't know how much of this has to do with the fear campaigns of the government, but I believe a combination of propaganda, and simple things like nature documentaries have contributed to this eco-friendly consciousness, as well of course as environmental emphasis in liberal education.

There is still a large problem that environmental consciousness has led many people to simply buy into carbon trading legislation and recycling programs as a solution to environmental problems. But in any case, people all over have changed many personal and shopping habits in the name of environmentalism.

My point here is that we seem to be doing better than we ever have regarding the environment. We care more, and we act more in favor of positive environmental trends. Currently, it is indeed cool to care. The government would surely love to take credit for this, but there must be many factors involved.

Even if governments of the past *were* responsible for the large part of the industrial revolution, and the modern counterpart, we would still be in a position to use all of what we have learned and change our underlying system of decision making and funding of public infrastructure and services.

Would we start to burn the forests down if "national park" status were lifted? I doubt it. Would we go out and shoot all the deer and eagles in a rampage? I doubt it. Would we start mining everywhere? Impossible.

It is worth mentioning that strip-mining the world would not be economical in any situation. Mining companies put great effort into selecting appropriate sites, because it is very easy to waste all of their money digging or drilling in the wrong places. They aim for efficiency because profitable mining is nearly impossible otherwise.

There are more *disused* mines in the world than there are mines in use, and this is the reason. It is easy to get the opposite impression when learning about mining in a government school – especially when mining for oil is included in the discussion.

Despite the fact that mining for everything from gold to silica to oil is cleaner and more efficient now than it ever has been, they portray the countryside as being essentially raped for its resources. Mining is the single most misrepresented industry on Earth. This misrepresentation is done in part by governments.

Watching a few hours of government sponsored environmental scare propaganda, we really can think that it is actually possible for mines and logging to destroy everything. This relies on our ignorance of the vastness of our territories, and an omission about the strident efforts that industry has taken to improve their practices over the past several decades. These efforts *have* paid off, but we are not told about it.

I live far up north among an ocean of trees. I often speak of the logging trucks as a common sight in my town – mining and logging are the only major industries. Usually I'm talking to a city person, and most often they gasp in some kind of dismay.

"Isn't that awful?" They say.

"No, not at all." I respond.

I don't know which letter to put in front of the "illions" to attempt to portray just how many trees there are in Canada. Zillions? According to the Ontario Forest Industries Association, there are currently 85 billion *harvestable* trees in the province – but there are many more smaller trees in the bush.

The Ontario forest is the size of Germany, Italy, and the Netherlands, combined. We have only cut small veins through the gigantic northern forest to build our little towns. Most of these towns exist around a mining operation, and beyond the narrow highways there are such vast stretches of forest that none of us can properly comprehend it.

We couldn't use that much paper or lumber even if we wanted to. We couldn't even burn it all before the first half grew back. The Ontario forest alone has more than 7 billion cubic meters of growing stock (tree volume) on harvestable land. Considering that the government owns 81% of forested land in the province, and 4% of the most productive forest is in protected parks, it is amazing that we still have 7 billion cubic meters of commercially-available wood products on the remaining 19% available forest.

Of course, most of that product is being cut from properties which are left to regrow in cycles – trees grow back, and within decades a plot of land is ready for another harvest. Most of the forest is not touched at all, and much of what has been developed is towns that you could blink while driving by and miss them completely. The roads and towns make little difference to the sheer size of the ocean of trees, and the logging is barely noticeable – mostly taking place on cheap land away from the main roads.

Logging has been happening in this area for well over 100 years, and yet the forests around our towns remain thick and vast. There aren't enough trucks to haul away the forest just outside of town. Our primitive trails on our undeveloped properties have to be maintained every year, or the bush will consume them.

The people who are trained to feign disgust at the thought of any mining or logging activity seem to have no better idea on what we should do. Should we not mine? Please explain how we would operate our modern world without mining. Type it on the smartphone or computer that requires precious metals such as gold that are mined in my town.

It is easy to be insulated from the realities of manufacturing, but the truth is that our society is built on mining activity. Logging is a tiny fraction of deforestation – vast tracts of land are cleared for biofuels, and logging for actual lumber is nothing in comparison to development.

As a society, we do use a lot of wood products, but not *that* much. Canada could probably supply the world with paper and it wouldn't dent the forest. By the time we cleared the first tenth of what we need, much of it would have grown back.

This is how logging works. But that is not what the government tells us. Actually they skip over much of this entirely. The result of this mis-education branded under environmentalism is a population ignorant to basic land use. They seem to suggest that either we don't use wood products at all, or that we simply don't do it in our countries.

The government does know how land use works. When we are upset about a new mining or logging development, or an airport being built, we are upset largely because of the liberal environmental focus in our schools and media. The Canadian government in particular always wants to make it look like it is on the side of environmental initiatives, but it it is also, clearly, perfectly aware of the importance of these industries, which is why it inevitably allows these developments.

If we do not log responsibly in our own countries, then countries such as China will do it for us and ship it to us on oil-based transport. This is not a solution to any part of our problem, if there even is a problem.

It is the same with mining. We have to get real about how our world works and how our technology works, instead of blindly giving in to environmental concepts that are inevitably sponsored by the government.

One of the most insane proposed "solutions" to the non-problem of wood use is "bioplastics." Instead of making durable goods from one of nature's finest materials (wood), or the less aesthetic yet still highly durable petrol-derived plastics, the indoctrinated naturalists propose that we use corn- and soy-based plastics, grown largely on newly-cleared, ex-rainforest land, and American farmland that could have been used to grow food.

This blows my mind. But it is a logical endpoint for those who believe the government's version of environmentalism.

When it comes to mining and logging, there is no problem. We are more efficient at these processes now than ever, and we have the ability to hold businesses accountable if they are acting irresponsibly. We are really only able to do this if these activities happen in our own countries.

If we believe these are problems that must be outsourced to some far away place, we most likely will do much more damage to the environment, and have no oversight of it. We can forget all about it as we sip our coffee from a bioplastic cup, thinking we have done some good in the world. The view is good from the high horse, but it is not reality.

Let's finish this chapter with recycling programs. These programs make us feel good, but in many cases – maybe most cases – these are simply a forced trash-sorting program. In many jurisdictions you face fines if you do not sort your "recyclables." Some places go further, forcing you to wash the waste before sorting it.

Labeling something "recyclable" does not mean that it actually gets recycled. In many or most cases, this sorting of trash is just a waste of our time and money. The stuff is delivered to a landfill or burned. It makes us feel good but it does nothing for the environment.

There is a simple solution to the problem of waste – use *less*. We can use less plastic, less packaging overall, and less cheap material goods that do not last as long as they could. Recycling does almost nothing to solve this.

Government "progress" is often measured on how much we produce (gross domestic product), yet many of the things we need to do to improve our world involve consuming *less*, not more. Thrift is a cultural virtue, and it is coincidentally terrible for GDP, which governments do not like to see lowered.[viii]

The only useful recycling programs I have ever seen are private companies that pay people for recyclable trash. 10 cents a bottle keeps bottles off the street. It really works. And we should still buy and use less of these single-use products anyway.

On the subject of littering, I have noticed a steady decline in civilian willingness to litter, and it is a great example of human education and prosperity leading to changes in environmentally-friendly behavior, having nothing to do with government. When I was growing up, littering was very normal, and our cities were filthy. In more recent years civilians everywhere seem to feel empowered to say something to those who litter, and this peer pressure has been a powerful motivator in changing behavior – it wasn't increased fines or policing that decreased littering.

Recycling requires a lot of energy, usually from sources that the liberal minds do not like. Recycling produces more demand for energy, and water. Recycled products are most often turned right back into wasteful single-use products.

Paper bags are also not the answer. These products also

consume massive quantities of energy and water – *more* than regular plastic bags, which are produced from what would otherwise be a waste product of oil refining. The answer will continue to be: use less, buy less.

One of the bigger fiascoes in my home city of Toronto was the "green bin" program. It has been called a wasted effort in major news outlets, and I would agree – except that it was much more than effort, it was also many millions of dollars.

We elected a "green" mayor. We were forced to pay for expensive new trash bins, a new type of green plastic bag to line these special bins, and a brand new system of trucks to collect the contents of these new bins and deliver it to where it needed to go.

This is in a city where we are already "strongly encouraged" to spend our own time sorting our trash into garbage and recyclables. Now we had to further sort our "organic" waste. Of course, it turns out that most of this effort was a complete waste of time and money for everyone, as this "green" waste was simply dumped into landfills, or trucked to Detroit to be burned.

Reportedly, some of the organic waste was turned into mulch for new playgrounds. "New playgrounds" sounds great, except that they were almost all built on top of old playgrounds that were perfectly fine except that the state deemed them unfit or unsafe.

The government didn't like the fun parts of the playgrounds. They had to use our money to tear them down and replace them with plastic, padded, "safe" versions that do not have any of those worrisome monkey bars or tire swings.

This mulch was apparently toxic to gardens, due to its high salt content. They had to do something with it, and this playground mulch was touted as an accomplishment.

This is fake environmentalism in action, ladies and gentlemen. Fake environmentalism is almost always a product of government.

Many governments do actually have useful environmental programs. This is not enough for me to say that government is good, or necessary. To my knowledge, our constitutions have nothing to do with the environment. Our governments are supposed to represent our interests, protect our rights and protect our society. It's great if they save some elephants, or protect breeding ground of endangered birds, but individuals and private groups do also protect lands, plant trees, and save animals.

On the subject of elephants, you might not know that the Toronto Zoo (owned by the government of Toronto), removed its elephants to a sanctuary after private activism led by celebrity Bob Barker condemned their inadequate treatment. We need government to protect species, except the ones they have in cages.

6. Business.

I have a biased opinion on this subject primarily because I am in a business that is actively suppressed by the government. This has become more relevant after 2020, because any time we attempt to share *any* information about the virus that was used as an excuse to shut down the world, or the stuff inside the needles that we are supposed to take to "go back to normal," government links appear on our posts.

Whatever we have to say about these very important topics, the government inserts itself, blocking out a portion of the screen in order to promote their version of sanctioned reality. This is an assault to free speech and information, it is bad for our business, and it is quite annoying.

I have mentioned some of the restrictions placed on our "alternative" health professions, and I don't need to repeat them. But there are many more. The government does indeed block many important compounds from getting to the open market. This ranges from practical items such as hemp, to potentially life-saving, artery-clearing medicines such as hawthorn berry extract.

I believe that humans are generally smart, and generally good. We are at least capable of hearing information about a product or substance, and making our own decision about whether to purchase or ingest it. Governments around the world do not believe this. They believe they must interfere in apparently every possible way with information about health, and products relating to that information.

It would be easy to insert a diatribe here about government sponsored alcohol, tobacco, and gambling, but I think that hypocrisy is evident enough already. I just don't think the average person realizes how much effort the governments of our industrialized countries put into suppressing natural medicines and supplements.

I wish I had some great number sets here for you, but I don't. I can only tell you from years of experience that when it comes to the health business, the government is our biggest obstacle.

Until 2020, the only time I had heard the word "lockdown" was in reference to a prison, or at school during an emergency drill – of course our public schools are basically organized in the same way as prisons. The spellcheck on my word processor does not recognize the word, yet this term has now become normalized for anyone living in this world police state. Our governments have introduced us to "rolling lockdowns," like rolling blackouts in underdeveloped countries.

These lockdowns have forced the closure of hundreds of thousands – probably millions – of businesses around the world. Small businesses are affected the most by these sanctions, while an elite group of "essential" businesses are allowed to continue operations in the "new normal."

I think this is bad for everyone, and I don't think I need to elaborate the point very much. My business operates mostly online these days, but we have definitely had to adapt to the reality that the average person either has less money, or more uncertainty about their future income than ever before.

We sell programs that our customers should expect to be

on essentially forever, so this lack of funds and uncertainty about future funds has greatly impacted the way we attract customers, and ultimately the average purchase price has decreased dramatically.

I have friends who have lost both their businesses *and* their hope of ever running a brick-and-mortar business again in my home country. I have seen cities I used to love boarded up because of this mess. All of this was caused by the government. Governments are the only entities capable of mass shut-downs and this type of forced bankruptcy.

In 2008 we experienced an event deemed "The Great Recession." There is a case to be made that government financial policies encouraged the initiation of the recession, but the bigger thing that many people had a problem with was the ensuing government "bailouts."

I had never heard the term "too big to fail" before this recession. My small business crashed during this time, in part due to the suddenly sunken economy. My mother had her mortgage rates change at this time – we lost our house and she went into bankruptcy. But the banks and some other "too big" businesses were given somewhere around 700 billion tax dollars to stay afloat.

I was one of many people who believed that these big businesses should be allowed to fail. I was brought up to believe that we lived in a "capitalist" country, and the market would determine whether a business succeeded or not. Government intervention was something more akin to communism. I still believe this. The companies who were bailed out – even if they eventually paid back the loans – did not deserve "public" support any more than the rest of us.

Governments support some businesses. They suppress others. There is no standard rules in place. They make things up as they go along. They play favorites and all of this is opposed to the concept of a "free market." The market will never be free until governments stop manipulating it at their whim.

Things can only be fair under some kind of standardized understanding. Governments either support all businesses (communism), or they support none of them (pure capitalism). Pure capitalism has never existed in any country in history. Governments have always intervened when they felt like it. Some people have always found this unfair. This system will never be fair until governments stop interfering with capitalism.

I don't want to go into a complicated analysis of how money is generated and assigned value. But I do believe that the overall system of currency, credit, and interest rates can call be handled by private businesses that are held accountable by the market. And if governments stopped interfering in massive ways like lockdowns and bailouts, we might be able to get on with business in peace.

There are many other significant difficulties created by the so-called nanny states who believe we are not capable of handling our businesses responsibly. The more "modern" your country or city is, the more taxes you will have to pay if you want to do business there.

These taxes come in the form mostly of licenses. You seem to need a license to do absolutely everything these days – and more such licenses and regulations are constantly being proposed by our Big Brother.

The government does not believe that consumers can monitor the quality of products, or food, or drinks. The government must oversee everything. Apparently quality business practices are accomplished by licenses and fees and outright taxes. You might wonder how paying for a license to do something makes it any safer or cleaner – I would be right there wondering with you.

Some industries do regulate themselves. Performance enhancing drugs are monitored in sports with a combination of private and public regulations. They have a pretty shoddy record, as there are many cases of famous athletes who had been doping for years, and claimed that in their sport PEDs were rampant. We spectators tend to wonder how an athlete can go so long without being caught. There is naturally talk of bribes and corruption and so on.

There is also much to be said and speculated when it comes to government regulations. Some industries seem to get away with anything while some are prevented from getting off the ground. Governments can be bribed and individuals in a government or a private body can be corrupt. In any case it seems we have a long way to go when it comes to monitoring unwanted behavior in both sport and industry.

In the age of social media many businesses are awakening to the new trend of transparency. I doubt that Coca-Cola will show us its overseas factories on social media, but overall we are much more aware of how businesses work.

How does government help us in terms of business? Unless you are a major corporation, I don't think they help us at all. They can provide small business loans, or subsidize them, but this can also be done by a private bank. As pro business as I am, I do not like the idea of government business loans. They have already done a terrible job with student loans, in my opinion.

Not all business ideas are good. Most businesses will fail, regardless of where funding comes from. Part of running businesses is learning from mistakes. Each venture carries unique risk. Banks are supposed to understand risk, which is why you are supposed to convince them of the merit of your venture before they agree to a loan. Governments look good when they "support" small businesses by providing funding, but what they are really providing are high-risk loans, at interest.

Some business models do require active debt to begin or maintain operations, but many small businesses do not. I do not know of any business gurus who advise starting a business by a loan, unless that loan is small and you have a definite plan to pay it in a reasonable time.

An argument is often constructed that business follows government. The "industrialized" nations are the ones that produce the most or the strongest businesses, they say. This is supposed to be a product of government stability affording a society to grow all types of wealth. I think this is nonsense. Businesses will be correlated to geography, resource availability, existing human intellectual capital, and all kinds of other factors. Governments just want credit for the whole cake recipe that produces innovation.

I recently read something interesting about the dramatic decrease in "productivity" in the Soviet Union when they switched from communism to capitalism. This might be the strongest business argument for government that I have seen to date, but I think it is a very tangled situation.

Shifting from totalitarianism to a semi-free market is bound to be a complicated picture. Having humans be "more productive" under the whip means practically nothing to me, as this measure says nothing about quality of life. I assume that they produced more under the gun than they would otherwise. I also assume that a generation raised in totalitarianism would have a hard time knowing how to run their own affairs.

Governments are known to inflate or deflate numbers when they want to make themselves look better. Businesses can do this too, to be fair. But I have every reason to believe that communist governments want to show more "productivity," and this is what they will show the world, regardless of reality.

Governments are not required for businesses to exist. Governments do not support most businesses. They often support harmful businesses such as junk foods and weapons and fake environmentalism. The rest of their participation in business is simply extortion via taxes and mafia-style "protection."

These taxes and strong-arm tactics are given innocent names like "regulation," and "national defense." I don't care what we call them, I believe these practices are bad for business.

The economic hardships imposed by government lockdowns worldwide are one of the clearest available examples of how governments can negatively impact business. Some might chalk this up to a once-in-a-lifetime occurrence, but we have no indication that this dystopia-in-the-name-of-health is anywhere near over.

There were and are no criteria to justify business closures — some of the most extreme lockdowns were and are still in places with very little actual effect from a virus, such as Australia and New Zealand. Governments everywhere have proven an enduring threat to business as we knew it.

7. Education.

The pandemic-induced lockdowns and forced closures of businesses also included schools in most industrialized countries. I believe that house arrest is bad for health, and I also believe the long-term school closures are very bad for education.

Lockdowns are obviously bad for the businesses that are forced to close. But the long-term closing of schools, to me, is a level of malice that I have not seen any modern government impose on its own citizens. Any existing issue I had with how governments actually run schools pale in comparison to my issue with schools being closed entirely.

In April of 2021, over a year after this fiasco started, the premiere of Ontario, Doug Ford, announced that schools would be closed "indefinitely." My spine still shutters as I write this more than three months later. "Outrageous" is not strong enough of a word.

Soon after, I made a post on social media that said:

"Closing schools in the name of health is a disgrace to both education and healthcare."

In the caption I said that "any politician who closed schools should be put in jail." If I wrote what I actually thought the punishment should be, I might have been kicked off of the platform.

I wasn't surprised that there were many comments to the effect of: "schools are terrible! They *should* be closed." I might once have made this argument, but I do believe it is far better to have inadequate schools than none at all.

I never liked school. I was a "good student," when I wanted to be, meaning that I got good grades when I chose to participate. But I never cared about any of it. School was a forced daily activity that I had to sit through until the bell rang.

It is interesting to think about the fact that wealthy people typically chose not to put their kids in government schools ("public" schools). They want to send their kids to "private" schools, operated by private businesses. Why? Because public schools apparently do a bad job at teaching kids – at least compared to private schools.

The most telling argument against government schools is probably the fact that when given a choice, people tend to choose private over public.

The public schools I attended felt closer to a prison system, or a training camp for factory workers. There were some good things about school, such as being around other kids, exposure to musical instruments, and even some of the actual curriculum I'm sure was useful. But I am convinced that the huge majority of the curriculum was a complete waste of time.

This won't be a thorough debate about the merits of teaching every kid in the world the quadratic equation or the Pythagorean theorem, but I think most of us can easily agree that much of what is taught to most kids will not help them in life.

Some kids will benefit from deep mathematical and systems teaching – the ones who enjoy this type of information will get more benefit from it and probably end up in an industry that uses systems-type thinking. Many kids will receive no benefit whatsoever from being forced to "learn" more than basic arithmetic, but they will endure a lot of stress about it for no reason at all.

Many of us will have no use for most of the academic concepts forced into us in public schools – and very little of it will even be remembered. Many of us will get no benefit from the memorize-and-regurgitate formula of "standardized education." Education is standardized because of government. They do not have the ability to monitor things that are not standardized. Standardization is good for government and bad for us.

In the book *Drive*, Daniel Pink argues in convincing detail that the keys to unlocking and sustaining intrinsic motivation are autonomy, mastery, and purpose. These concepts are entirely absent from today's standardized education. The only school-based activities which might encourage children to harness their inborn power to motivate themselves are *extra*curricular, i.e. things that are not required to graduate. These are the sports teams and art clubs and so on that have nothing to do with the actual school curriculum.

More problems come up when a government believes things like, every 8 year old should learn about things like sex. This is yet another effect of government centralization, because otherwise this would be an isolated problem in the few schools who thought this was appropriate. But this could be any subject – do we really believe that the government is always correct in what it teaches and how it teaches it? I doubt any educator on Earth would support total government control, or total standardization of education.

Diversity of teaching and opinion is a good thing, and it is diversity that acts as the best regulator. People who are taught different things can bring these different perspectives and data together to form new ideas and opinions. If we are all taught the same thing there is really no way to monitor mistakes or encourage debate – what could there be to debate, as we were all taught "the truth," right?

If one school teaches sex to 8 year olds while others do not, parents can choose which school they would like their children to attend. When everything is standardized, there is no choice.

We will never all agree on exactly what form education should take, or which subjects and concepts should be taught or ignored. I just don't trust the government to handle this responsibly.

My mother is a teacher, and I actually jeopardize her career by even mentioning her here because our government can fire her for speaking out against the school system. She has told me many times that it bothers her that she has to teach children things she believes are incorrect. She has absolutely no freedom to bestow her worldly wisdom on her pupils. She is completely chained to the standardized curriculum.

There is no such thing as a standard child. The government does us an enormous disservice to insist on standardizing human activities. When they give us health guidelines for "average" people, they are harming the great majority of the population who do not fit the description of their average person. It is the same with education. There are gifted kids and special needs kids; there are kids more interested in art and those more interested in maths. This diversity could be a good thing, if the government did not insist on standardizing as much as possible.

There are some things that would indeed benefit everyone to learn in school – things such as money management, investment, and business operations can be just as technical as algebra, yet these things will actually definitely come up in every adult life. Financial illiteracy is rampant and probably has something to do with its absence from standardized curriculum.

We are probably all going to disagree slightly on what material is best for our children to learn. This disagreement offers us the opportunity to customize education in different places and for different types of children. This diversity, in my opinion, is an excellent way to fortify our cultures with a variety of knowledge and skills.

In other words, having more flexible education – *not* standardized – would be great for our society. It would likely be much more enjoyable for the children as well. Maybe they wouldn't feel like they are in a prison learning useless things at gunpoint.

Next there is the issue of behavior. I was one of the bad kids, as were my friends. We all got regular detentions and suspensions and most of us eventually got expelled from school. I don't feel that I ever properly integrated into society, and I can say that my anti-socialization was probably in part due to the school system that I eventually disdained.

School taught me, first and foremost, that I did not want to be a part of society. This is a terrible outcome for any kid.

There is a vicious cycle involved here. The kid who gets in trouble almost automatically annoys the adults who have to sit us down, give us a speech, and ultimately punish us. Each such incident makes them less happy to deal with us, we pick up on the subtle cues that we are indeed the bad kids, and we can begin to play into that role as a self-fulfilling prophecy.

Bad kids are made worse the further they go into the system. My friends who were punished harshly – such as being expelled younger than myself, or sent to a juvenile jail or military school – unanimously ended up far worse than me. By "worse" I mean, more aggressive, less trusting, and more likely to *stay in the system.*

None of us were successfully reformed by punishment. And there was no reward available to bait us into good behavior. They didn't have anything to offer us. It would not be effective to bribe us with goods, even if that were possible. What we really wanted and needed, I think, was a structure that encouraged us to build useful skills instead of useless algebra and boring, sanitized history.

The bad kids like me were typically more "hands-on" types of people. We couldn't sit still and didn't want to. There was no punishment or reward that would get us to do the standard curriculum "properly." We just didn't care enough.

I ended up in media production in the field of health advocacy and related product sales. It is very hands-on. Nothing I ever learned in school matters for my current position in society – media production is a specialty normally reserved for "higher" education, which I did not pursue, and neither "alternative" health, nor sales or business are available courses in regular public education.

Most of my friends ended up in the trades. Many of them do excellent professional hands-on work. Some of them didn't "make it out," and spent their lives on drugs instead of doing anything productive.

Not one of my "bad" friends went to university. I even worked at a university for a time in my life – doing hands-on work – yet I never graduated from any post-secondary education.

My estimate is that my friends and I could have just skipped primary school after perhaps the first grade, and high school entirely. We gained nothing there. We had some fun and made some friends, but we did not learn anything other than a hostility for structured authority.

Though I did not enjoy school, it was there that I picked out the first books to read on my own. Access to a library was definitely the best thing that school ever did for me, but of course this did not have to happen at school. When they began closing schools across the world, one of my biggest concerns was that children wouldn't have access to books.

Many of us tend to forget how many short books we read in the early years of school. In the later years we don't tend to get the scheduled library time. In my opinion, this early exposure and encouragement to read is crucial. I have no idea where I would be without books, and I have no idea what the children of today will fill their minds with in the future if they fail to develop the habit of reading early because their schools and libraries are closed.

These days it is said often that CEOs tend to read around 60 books a year, and I would agree that there is a strong correlation between success and study. We are told in school that it is *more school* that will be the key to success, but I think reading takes precedence.

Back to the post at the start of this chapter, you can see why I might have once agreed that just shutting down the schools could be a good thing. We hated it, so why not shut it down?

Because kids are not all the same, and neither are parents. Some parents choose to homeschool their children instead of enrolling them in public school. I think this is a great option, especially if they do not have access to private school. But this requires a commitment and level of patience that parents are not required or likely to possess.

I do not know if I have the patience or understanding to competently school a child myself. Glancing around the adult environment, I imagine there are very few who are fully capable of handing this responsibility. This is fine – I run a business, why should I be expected to also be great at being a homeschool teacher?

This brings us to my point about closing schools being a disgrace. It is because we adults are not all capable of doing a good job at teaching. There is a type of professional that goes to school to learn how to teach – we call these professionals "teachers." I am not a teacher and chances are, neither are you. *This is why we pay this profession.*

For all of human history, teaching has been a thing that adults did in the same room as their pupils. There is no precedent for "remote" learning, and so we can have no confidence that any learning will even take place under this dramatic shift in format. I remember being frustrated about checking my college grades on the computer, and I can't imagine kindergartners spending their whole day on devices.

I work indoors, mostly on a computer. Forcing a complete shift from classroom to "remote" is akin to forcing me to suddenly do my work outside. You might say, well this is better for my health – and maybe it would be. But I can come up with a long list of inconveniences this would produce. I think it is best if we can choose our own work environments, and I will bet that teachers, parents, and students will all, by a large majority, choose "in person" learning over "remote."

Homeschool is not "remote" learning. Homeschool is in--person and hands-on. I am convinced that there is no such thing as "remote learning." I have watched some of this farce first hand and I cannot believe that anyone thinks it is a good idea to put kids of all ages on computers and tablets and expect them both to actually learn the curriculum *and* not mess around on the internet.

That second point might be the biggest challenge. To fully ensure the child is actually doing what they are supposed to be doing, you need to watch them. I run a business, and like many adults overseeing this remote learning nonsense,

I have many other things to do than hover over the kids to make sure they're not on some other website or app.

Kids are very clever. They are committed and tenacious and they seem to do a very good job at sneaking around what they are supposed to be doing and finding ways to pretend they are actively engaged with the remote learning. It is a lot of work and evidently a lot of headache for the average parent to now act as supervisor for their child.

Keep in mind that these children are already being "taught" by a paid professional – and now on top of that they largely require unpaid supervision by the parents. If this is a public school situation, our tax dollars pay for that professional, yet the teacher is handicapped to actually ensure the child is watching the screen.

I can only imagine how stressful this is for people who do not work from home – many probably have to hire a baby-sitter. I work from home and it is excessively annoying just to have to hear the combat between my wife and her kids about this remote learning thing. I said that an inadequate school is better than no school – but only as long as this takes place offline.

On top of that, I believe that the kids who are now growing up in this forced remote learning environment are slowly becoming socially retarded. I am deeply fearful of what the world will be like when this generation reaches adulthood. Almost everything I learned in my school years had some-thing to do with being punched in the arm or given a dirty look by another kid if I did or said something socially unac-ceptable. I do not believe that screens can teach our chil-dren any of the most valuable lessons in life.

This goes for face coverings and plastic barriers as well. Children, especially babies, do need to see the face in order to connect it with the words and emotions of the speaker. Someone who doesn't understand the emotional connection to speech might come across as a psychopath. Children need to play together closely to form the bonds that will become the basis of their emotional experience in life outside of the home. Instead, government mandates are causing children to be separated, fearful, and largely inactive as a result of all of this. In places where children *are* in actual schools, they are largely being separated and covered. I don't feel too dramatic to say that as these mandates continue, childhoods are literally being stolen by the government.

Completely left out of the mainstream conversation is a growing belief that electromagnetic frequencies from wireless electronic devices are *harmful*, particularly to children. Whether this is true or not, the government imposition of this style of electronic teaching forces children to use these potentially harmful devices. This completely eradicates parental decision to expose their children to this risk.

Many parents do still choose to keep their small children off of the internet, to shield them from many of the inappropriate things they could stumble onto or search deliberately. Remote learning has made this nearly impossible.

I watched my mother do some remote learning sessions with kindergarten children recently, and I felt a deep pity for those kids. They are supposed to be finger painting and simply learning to play nicely with each other and interact respectfully with the teacher, not being forced to navigate video-chat portals and electronic learning modules – I don't even think I can do that effectively! Of course, much of the school day is lazily filled up with videos that are supposedly educational, and each of these kids has to be individually supervised by an adult in the room with them.

I do not think the Ontario government will allow these children to attend a real school any time soon. The time we spend playing in the sandbox and finger painting is the same time we learn the basics of getting along with people.

It is heart wrenching to think that these children will spend their most important learning years in this electronic bubble.

To the main points of this book, governments across the world fail our children by education. In the first place, we do not require governments to host schools. In the second place, governments often come up with bad ideas for education that should not be done. Teaching little kids about sex is only one example, and that is rather innocuous compared to some of the more egregious distortions of facts taught in public schools.

If a few private schools didn't believe a historical event happened, for example, it would not be a big deal because it would be an isolated occurrence. But when governments decide how history should be written, we are simply at their mercy. Kids everywhere are taught the same nonsense only because governments control schools.

I do not believe any private enterprise would be capable of the level of indoctrination we can experience through government schools. Governments are the only entities large enough and powerful enough to implement society-wide indoctrination. Not only can private businesses do just as good a job, or better, at teaching than the government, private businesses are incapable of brainwashing on a mass scale.

If all schools were private, what would happen to the families who can not afford it? I don't propose to have every answer here in this book, but I will say that I would be happy to see an overall decrease in government size and power, rather than a full decommissioning.

If governments actually only oversaw the finances and basic plans for roads and education, I would not have enough reason to write this book. It is the fact that they fail us *and* do us harm that prompts this dramatic essay. I do believe that I would have been better with no school than with the government schools I attended – even though I still strongly believe that a bad school is better than no school.

There isn't much of an option to have "no education." The kids like myself who ditched school and dropped out got plenty of educational opportunities out there in the world. It is worth considering that many of the giants in the history of science and academia attended schools that bear almost no resemblance to what we have today, and spent much less time in them.

Today we do need specialized education if we want to be in certain professions, such as medicine, engineering, or teaching. But there are also lists of businesses and professions that do not require formal education.

In the past, most kids only had a small bit of formal education. The rest they learned on the farm or in the factory or on their business ventures. I do believe that wider access to education is a good thing, but that still does not make it necessary for every child to attend school k-12. I could have dropped out in grade 3 since there was nothing useful taught in the later years. But engineers, doctors, nurses, scientists, electricians, and many other professions do require several extra years of specialized education and training.

I would support a government scale that still accommodated public schools for those families who could not afford private education. But I would also argue that if the government didn't control the economy, there wouldn't be as many people reliant on government handouts such as public school.

In Chapter 10, *Police*, I will argue further that government welfare actually creates the dependent lower classes who would need public education.

Here in the education chapter it is worth mentioning that many governments are known to have put quite massive effort and money into spreading disinformation. One of the more famous instances of this was in the USA, known as "Operation Mockingbird."

In the 1950's journalists and others in media were recruited to disseminate government-sponsored propaganda. It was only in 1967 that the whistle was blown on this operation, and the program was officially ceased. I think we are fools to believe that this was the last instance of deliberate government misinformation.

On top of clandestinely spreading misinformation, the government also spends some of its "research and development" budget on learning more about human psychology – presumably in order to further manipulate it.

In 2016 the US government spent 3.2% of the 66.2 billion dollar federal research funding, on psychological research. This is only one aspect of funding that goes directly against our wellbeing, and we will further explore this subject in the next chapter.

8. Research & Development.

Now we come to one of the more obvious misuses of "public" money. Governments across the world have a strange obsession with R&D that is blatantly antagonistic to human welfare.

Governments love to spend our money on weapons development, and this can be in the form of traditional crafts and projectiles, or more sophisticated "bio" weapons such as modified viruses. Enormous sums are spent on newer and better ways to kill more people. Vast sums are also spent on "non-lethal" weapons, such as sonic frequency weapons.

I am not against weapons. I think we should all have the right to own weapons, and all human populations have a right to defend themselves. I also think there should be few or no government restrictions on businesses choosing to specialize in weapons R&D.

My problem is with the government paying for this. Private enterprise is fully capable of innovation corresponding to market demand. If the market demanded more sophisticated lethal or non-lethal weapons, the private market would have no problem supplying this.

If private businesses were all allowed to research and develop anything they wanted, wouldn't they all just create more and more powerful weapons? I must remind all of us that governments are the ones who insist on researching and developing ever more powerful weapons. They are the ones who wanted nuclear weapons, biological weapons, and even digital disruptions such as electromagnetic pulse weapons.

One of the things the government does very well is to convince the people that they are tremendously powerful. We see the stealth bombers and guided missiles and we justifiably assume that the government has unmatchable powers of destruction. But I do think they are also inclined to exaggerate their powers. Wouldn't we be crazy to revolt against our almighty government?

I am part of a growing group of skeptics who believe that nuclear weapons are a myth created and perpetuated by governments. It is actually very difficult to prove that nuclear weapons technology exists at all. There is no visible difference between supposedly nuked cities like Hiroshima or Nagasaki, and fire-bombed cities like Tokyo or Dresden.

My working theory is that the whole nuclear thing is made up simply as an old-school intimidation tactic. Lesser governments like North Korea are either in the know about the farce, or they are spending large sums in complete vain. When North Korea claims it has or is close to nuclear ability, the major powers must publicly entertain this as a real possibility – lest their own farce be known to the world. I tend to think they know about the hoax, because they also claim to have a space program, but we will get to that.

Even if nuclear weapons are real, it is unlikely that private businesses would be very interested in this avenue of R&D. From what we are told about nuclear weapon development, it is excessively expensive. Governments are happy to spend money with no hope of returns, but private companies are not so keen to waste money. If DuPont or 3M or Lockheed Martin was interested in nukes, they would have no way to profit from their labor when it is complete – not to mention the fact that some companies such as Lockheed, only exist in their current form because of government contracts. The only entities they could sell such weapons to are governments – there are no criminal organizations that come even close to being able to afford nukes.

One of the main arguments that comes up here among those who believe in nuclear weapons is that "we have to do this, or the other governments will!" We must empower our government to develop horrible weapons, or else some other governments will do it anyway. This is fear-based thinking at its finest.

History is presented to us as a list of empires and conquests, and we assume that this trend would simply continue no matter what. We might as well have a government determined to research and develop weapons forever, because humans just love destroying and conquering each other. I don't believe this version of history, but even if it were true, there is no reason to believe that any army would be able to conquer our modern world by force.

They couldn't conquer Vietnam by force, and in the news this week is the current capture of the Afghanistan parliament by the Taliban, which marks the end of a failed 20 year joint campaign of American, Canadian, United Kingdom and other troops. Russia occupied Afghanistan for 10 years from 1979-1989, and also failed to conquer the territory. We might be a bit softer in North America, but we are also armed and able to defend our own sovereignty.

The most ardent conspiracy theorists will usually not claim that governments are interested in subduing us by force. The book *1989* is not about a population subdued by force – it is one subdued by propaganda and the *threat* of force, amid an everlasting war overseas. It is obvious that the preferred method of domination is subliminal and non-violent. Governments have already conquered us without force. The *threat* and *fear* of force has proven sufficiently powerful to control us. They use force against non-compliant "lesser" nations, but by far the most conquering is done with propaganda, not force.

Sometimes the government comes out with a technology that does actually benefit us. People love to say "but without the government we wouldn't have the internet!" I think this is another nonsense straw-man argument. I believe we would have converged on the internet either way – there were many parallel developments leading to what would eventually be the internet that had nothing at all to do with government research or contracts.

It also seems like the government does not have an interest in sharing the fruits of their R&D unless someone blows the whistle and draws attention to the invention. I don't think we would ever have known about the stealth bomber if it weren't for inside leaks. I doubt they would have given us the internet if they had the ability to contain it.

Alas, it is not a long list of useful things that have come from government-funded research. We have paid an unbelievable amount of money for these few innovations, and most of them are still nothing more than fancy, expensive weapons. This research could have come from private universities and mega businesses like DuPont or 3M. There is plenty of profit to be made from innovative products and services, and the free market is already naturally incentivized to undertake R&D.

Then there is the unknowable list of things we will never have access to *because* the R&D was conducted in secret. Governments seem to hate transparency. They do not like their populations knowing how they spend the R&D money. We don't know if this money was wasted or harmful or if it was beneficial – and we will probably never know, because the government likes to take our money and bury it.

One of the other large categories of government-funded

R&D is pharmaceutical "medicine." Any compound designed to "treat" a disease or symptom is automatically called a medicine.

Most people do not know that the only pharmaceutical medicines that have ever cured any diseases are antibiotics – and the golden age of this R&D is far behind us. The peak of antibiotic R&D was in the 1950's, and there has not been a new class of antibiotic drugs discovered since 1987. It would not have mattered who paid for antibiotic research, it would eventually have been done and we would be in the same position we are now, with a solid list of antibiotic products.

In any case, we are still faced with the problem of antibiotic resistance. If anything, governments prioritizing pharmaceutical R&D over "alternative" treatments has resulted in an over-reliance on this one type of drug. This over-reliance has resulted in populations which are now more resistant to antibiotics.

Since the government only officially recognizes allopathic medical schools as legitimate practitioners of medicine, we can all be forgiven for missing the tremendously important point that *diseases are not caused by drug deficiencies.* 100% of the research money used for "chemotherapy" or other pharmaceutical interventions to degenerative diseases has been wasted.

No cancer research center or diabetes foundation or muscular dystrophy association or any other group studying any other degenerative disease will ever come across a cure under the allopathic belief system. They will never cure cancer with drugs because cancer is not caused by a lack of drugs. It does not matter if governments or private enterprises fund this type of research, it is categorically useless.

Given that our food system is only set to have *less* nutrients in the supply next year than this year, we expect the incidence of all degenerative diseases to *increase*, regardless of how much money is thrown at these problems by way of pharmaceutical R&D.

These problems are completely solvable, but in our modern world ruled by governments, we will probably never have any money spent on the things that will actually prevent and reverse diseases. These preventative practices have already been implemented in the animal industries with tremendous success. We have had a hundred years to witness the miracle of preventative nutrition in animals, and there is no democratic government in the world actively interested in applying this to humans.

To contradict myself slightly, I will mention that the Chinese government does indeed force certain supplementation in certain areas of their country. Since the government has to pay for all of the healthcare, it is in its interest to prevent diseases wherever possible. Theoretically this should be the case in Canada as well, where healthcare is government controlled.

Of course I will not concede the trade-off between communist domination and free supplements. We can pay for our own supplements and prevent our own diseases, and I do not trust the government to make the best choices – I only trust myself to make those choices. China forcing selenium supplementation might be beneficial for those who receive it, but this benefit does not outweigh the cost of totalitarianism, and of course the Chinese government could equally start to force other substances under the same pretense of "for your own good."

The animal industries have eliminated every disease and birth defect you can name. These industries funded the research largely by themselves, though some of it was indeed government money. The problem is, this information was only applied to animals. Humans still get the same diseases that were completely eliminated in livestock a hundred or a thousand years ago. Unless governments totally reverse the type of medicine it considers legitimate, there will be no serious progress toward better human health or longevity.

The United States of America is a great example of R&D gone wrong. The USA spends more than the rest of the world *combined* on high-tech and pharmaceutical-centric "healthcare," and yet in 2021 they rank 46th in longevity out of all the nations in the world. R&D has not helped in any measurable way. Government funding has done nothing to prevent the plagues of heart disease or diabetes or cancer, and unless governments change their opinion on nutrition, it never will.

Out of the 45 countries who do better on longevity than the R&D-heavy America, several of them are third-world nations with very little money to invest in any type of R&D. They cannot afford sophisticated weapons any more than they can afford sophisticated medical equipment.

You might be surprised to learn that Cuba, Estonia, Lebanon, and even French Guiana outrank America in health and longevity. This clearly suggests that R&D is irrelevant to the health and longevity of the people.

Research is definitely expensive. Currently it is estimated that around 50% of all research is funded by governments. This percentage has decreased in recent decades as private corporations are increasing their share of worldwide R&D – particularly pharmaceutical research.

Most R&D from all sources is still focused on weapons and drugs. Governments are not necessary to undertake this research, and it is easy to argue that most of this is obviously harmful.

Other than governments, it is really only major companies who can undertake meaningful research and development. Interestingly, one of the few agreed roles of government is to prevent corporate monopolies. I am not going to argue that monopolies are good, I am just pointing out that if Bell or AT&T were not broken up by governments, they would have a lot more power to do R&D in their fields.

One of the main things governments are given credit for creating is the internet – a web-based communications system. It is reasonable to assume that the giant "monopolies" of telecommunications could or would have produced the internet if they were allowed to do their business without interference.

It puzzles me that our modern culture is reflexively against corporate monopolies, yet we skip right over the fact that the largest monopolies are governments themselves. It is as if the mafia has convinced us that street gangs exceeding five members are a threat to humanity – and of course we must pay the mafia to keep us safe from this threat.

Governments monopolize our finance and credit systems, our education, and ultimately our economy, since they bully some businesses and promote others at their whim. For most of the last century governments have also monopolized R&D, and the result was a lot of expensive weapons and not much more.

I do not want to add too many conspiracies to this book, but there is one more that I would like to mention here. One of the biggest science fiction myths of all time is the "spaceship Earth." It is said that since we are destroying our planet, we are going to have to "find another."

For one thing, it would presumably cost less to fix our own planet than to "terraform" another. For another thing, there are many people, including myself, who do not believe there is sufficient evidence to declare that any other planets, or even space itself, actually exists. Some readers will not find this shocking, but those who think we have just gone off the deep end are the ones who believe the model of the world presented by the government.

NASA says that they have spent around 650 billion dollars since their inception, but this does not include any of the secret space-related projects. The current annual NASA budget is around 20 billion US dollars, and they spend far more than any other country. That is over 60 million dollars a day. *If* space does not exist, this is an absolute abomination. If it *does* exist, we have received absolutely nothing of practical value for this investment.

In this case it wouldn't matter whether the money came from governments or private businesses, because it seems to be a myth that we can exit this world through the sky. Private companies have eagerly thrown themselves in the modern "space race," and they have wasted every dollar they have spent.

No one who has purchased a "ticket to space" will ever get value for that money – apparently, after many years of waiting, many refunds have been demanded. These people will not go to space because they cannot go to space. Most private and public visions of space travel have quieted down and are no longer making bold claims about civilians accessing space any time soon.

I am writing this mere days after billionaire Jeff Bezos filmed some high altitude "zero-G" footage and released a very CGI (computer generated image) looking video of a rocket that looked like a phallus. The conspiracy community seems to agree that this is simple mockery. My primary problem here is with government agencies pretending to go to space at our expense. I don't know how many people take Bezos' penis rocket or Elon Musk's space car seriously, but I just take them as a bad joke.[ix]

The private space exploration company Virgin Galactic, after almost 17 years since its inception in 2004, and over 500 million dollars invested, has only reached around 86 kilometers elevation. Presumably this is close to the limit of what is possible, as they say that space starts around 100 kilometers above us.

So, if we cannot physically go to space, why do our governments show us "proof" of such ventures? Excellent question, and I can only speculate the answer.

My working theory is that the Russians were the first to discover the impenetrable barrier above. They could have announced this, but they chose to propel the myth that they are indeed participating in a "space race." At some point the USA must also have learned about the barrier, and also chose to create the theater show instead of tell the truth. This is how North Korea can also claim to have a space program with varying success – it is very difficult for the higher powers to call them out on it, lest their own fraudulent programs be revealed.

This is possibly the most expensive fiction we have ever paid for. If the American people or any population knew that their government was spending billions of dollars on an entirely fake industry, we would probably be quite upset.

Whether space is real or not, we the people have received absolutely no benefit from any space-related R&D. I believe we have only paid for mildly entertaining computer graphics and science fiction. Having once believed in space, I do feel like I have been slapped in the face by our governments who have sold us extremely expensive cartoons and fake science. People who care about truth and technological progress will doubtless feel similar dismay if they come to believe that everything we have been told about space is a lie.

Of course this is a conspiracy theory, and I cannot prove a negative, but it should be very easy to prove that space is real, if it were actually real. We wouldn't believe zoologists if they claimed to discover a new species yet showed us only cartoons – and we would probably be very hesitant to hand the zoology department billions of tax dollars for further cartoons. At some point we would probably ask for real proof. But since governments monopolize education, we are taught that the cartoons and computer graphics are real.

This is only one of the many conspiracy theories involving government that is worthy of research. I would like to elaborate more but this is not the place for it. My only intention is to highlight the fact that the supposed greatest achievements of government-funded R&D are not even clearly real discoveries. If they really are lies, these are among the largest lies ever told.

9. Art.

Governments have always had a mixed relationship with art and artists. As with business, governments tend to support some artists, and suppress others.

It has been said that art funded by government is simply propaganda, and I would agree. As an artist myself, it is hard for me to say that funding for arts can be negative, but I really don't think their involvement is good for anyone involved.

I probably have very little chance of getting any government money. Government support is usually for very specific projects and often those that can be displayed publicly. If I do get a grant, I will be highly controlled in what I can actually produce with this money.

Some governments support the arts more than others, but generally it is a very small part of their role. Governments are willing to spend seemingly endless money on weapons and war, yet they dole out pennies for artists and expect very strict returns. They want their country and the rest of the world to see how great their artists are, and it does seem to be mostly about the show, not the art.

Government-approved art is usually sanitized and sterile. Unless it was painted a long time ago, governments are generally hostile to free expression. I realize this may sound more emotional than factual, but these opinions are hard to show numbers for.

At the public schools I attended I was always disappointed by the lack of art education or training in the curriculum. We all had to be tested on the quadratic equation and the bogus version of history we were taught, yet art was essentially treated as less important than recess. I don't remember having any serious scrutiny of my technique, or learning anything at all about art theory or history.

The government could not be bothered to hire actual artists to teach art in public schools – regular teachers handled the art class. The result was a farce in which we glued dry noodles to cardboard and called it "art".

We had an actual musician teaching our music class for a while, and we learned the basics of reading music and music history. When this teacher left – to teach at a private art school, of course – we were given another general teacher who knew nothing about music. This is the norm in public schools, and it is an utter waste of time and money – instruments are quite expensive, and there is nothing to be learned from someone who does not know how to use them.

Someone might argue that this is not necessary to learn in school, and I would retort that learning the quadratic equation is not necessary for most, except for those who go on to become teachers who must teach the quadratic equation. I will bet that a large portion of readers will actually have already searched "the quadratic equation" when I first mentioned it because they had completely forgotten it, proving its irrelevance to our lives.

Art is what makes life worth living. Art is just as necessary as math, science, and engineering – anyone who disagrees should not be caught listening to music or watching a film.

Governments treat art like a tool, as if it were gross domestic product. A lot of art makes the government look good, but that is all. Since this is the only benefit the government gets from art, this is as far as the support goes. And since quantity is more important to the government than quality, we have "enough" sterile art to appease the quota. They hand out some money, they hold up the sanctioned art, and that is all. This really isn't the type of education, career incentive, and cultural environment necessary for a rich art subculture.

One reason that art is great is because it costs so little to teach and produce it. All that is required is some basic exposure and instruction. After the basics, it does not require rote learning, or tedious drills, or tests. All of the normal measures of "standardized" education are not necessary for art. Maybe this is one reason it is not taken seriously by government education: it is very hard to measure and grade.

It is even harder to measure the benefit that art and artists give to their world, but it is definitely very valuable – I doubt any sane person would proclaim to want to live in a world without art.

Governments profess to care about a few key things – "sustainable development," increasing taxes, and to be honest I really don't know what else they are interested in other than sustaining their own careers and possibly, world domination. It is hard to find many government representatives anywhere in the modern time or throughout history who had a serious priority to promote the arts in their country.

There are exceptions, especially in Europe, where artists and writers were treated with very high acclaim and art academies for painting and sculpting and performance and so on were supported to various degrees. I don't think this was really a product of government as much as governments working with an already rich culture and history of art production and appreciation.

Most governments have art collections. They keep them in museums, and many countries even allow their citizens to visit these museums for free. This is simply not a necessary function of the government – private people and organizations are completely capable of collecting art and showing it publicly.

I recently visited an excellent showcase of historical paintings at the Houston Museum of Fine Arts. Admission was free[1] because of a corporate sponsor, which to many people seems to be part of "the enemy" - Shell Oil Company. The lead corporate sponsor for the exhibition was another controversial company, JP Morgan Chase & Co., and most of the paintings were on loan from private individuals, which has long been custom in the showing of art at major galleries. Though there are many excellent museums and collections owned by governments, it is just not necessary for them to be involved.

Some of the biggest and greatest art collections in the world have historically been owned by churches, and this is still true today. Churches and popes and other representatives of religion have been the most consistent patrons of the arts in history. I've even done work for the church, and they paid well and promptly. Surely this support has also been largely for the purposes of a form of propaganda, but there is at least the hint of a spiritual benefit acknowledged in the process.

Many artists have also believed at some point in their careers that they were doing God's work. Many of them lived long, determined lives, and left their legacy to us hundreds of years later, still providing awe and inspiration and lessons about form and subject and technique.

---

1   Thursdays only!

I only bring this up because in my modern education I was supplied with a great deal of formal animosity for the church. I am not religious at all, but I do feel that religions are far more interested in the arts than governments, and my government school pushed me away from spirituality very explicitly – we are made to feel dumb for believing anything other than the government's version of the world. Government schools taught me that the church is ignorant and wasteful and will ultimately probably fade from human priority – yet the ignorant creationists have supported art through hundreds of years of changing governments and empires.

Both churches and governments have burned paintings and books, and both use art for their own political agendas, though at least the religious world has continued to support the strive for *excellence* in art. I have actually heard, many times, someone say that some piece of abstract art, or a bad film, or unpleasant music, was an *insult* to God.

Today, governments tend to support art *programs* instead of individual artists. Individual artists can also apply to and be approved for entry to a program or to receive a grant. In the past, when individual patrons such as popes or dukes or queens wanted a portrait or a mural or a Madonna, they sought out the best artists of the day for the commission.

I wouldn't want the government spending any tax time on choosing which artists to support, but I do think that money for art should be much more selective than it tends to be when it is spent in government programs. Let me explain.

When the patrons of the day select the finest artists, there are numerous benefits. The patron gets to enjoy excellent art, the artist tends to get paid top dollar, and the collectors and museum-goers of the future have what we call masterpieces to enjoy for centuries. This is, in essence, a career opportunity which artists of the day can hope to attain by climbing the commission ladder and improving their work.

Our rich history of art is largely due to the history of patrons commissioning individual artists. Today the situation is much different. Sometimes governments do pay individual artists to make something, like a statue or a mural, or to perform at a festival. But generally their art money goes into programs, where many people have the opportunity to attend a class, a series of classes, a summer camp, or some kind of festival activity.

The problem with these types of activities, though they can be great for communities and a lot of fun for the children, they hardly contribute to mastery of a technical skill. I did take an art class at a government recreation center once, and I did some art activities at various festivals. They were fun. But mastery tends to require years of disciplined instruction and/or practice. Short-term government programs don't do much to support the type of training that one would need to truly become a professional artist.

These activities do not support or promote a strive for excellence – just finish the activity and go home with the participation trophy. These class or activity based programs might encourage some people to pursue art further, but there is generally no talk of careers. Activity art is closer to hobby crafts – pitched as fun or as a way to get away from it all, not as a serious career path.

At real art schools I am sure there are teachers there who have made a good living from their art, but I have not seen this in government-funded programs. There is a distinct lack of masters, and so these programs tend to be closer to play-time, hosted by people who probably wanted to be artists, but have never been very successful with it.

In the past, great artists tended to inevitably have spent time working in the studio of a master, or at least somebody who was very good and was producing work for a ready market. As you were learning how to do art, you were also learning about the art market, buyer preferences, traditions in form and subject and so on. You learn a lot more than "how to paint a landscape 101." Governments don't have to have much to do with this, but if children are legally obliged to be in school, they must complete their grades before devoting seriously to anything else.

Above I mentioned that much of the finest art we have on record was produced from the finest artists of the time being paid top dollar for their effort. This meant that one could strive for excellence and hope to be compensated excellently in the end. The vast majority of the people who utilize government art programs will not become a professional artist, or ever be well compensated for however much practice they end up putting in.

In other words, when art funding goes into art programs, it does not really go to artists. The funding is for the public, and at best it can stimulate interest in art. Real artists are produced by years of purposeful effort, and they make real money from commissions and sales, not from art programs.

In public schools and activity programs, kids probably wont be exposed to any examples of success in the field of visual arts. Googling the richest artists of today doesn't help much, as they are a tiny minority, and the market landscape they came up in is much different from today. If you want to be successful as an artist, you will have to study how to do that, and come up with a plan pretty much on your own.

A common criticism against politicians is that their primary interests tend to stretch only as far as their term is scheduled to be. 4 year term presidents have incentive to look good during that time. They might not be so concerned about the debt left to the next administration, or whether the projects they promoted will have enduring value. It is similar with art programs. The government does look good when it sponsors art programs, but there is really no effort in place to support serious art training.

It is not necessary for any formal institutions to support the arts. It would be great if there were more support, but it is not required. What *is* required for art and artists to thrive, I believe, is *freedom*, and I would argue that the biggest threat to freedom everywhere is the dominance of governments.

Whether it is public or private, serious art development requires a lot of devoted time, and like "raw science," art does require a lot of freedom and flexibility in the whole process from learning to training to producing. It just doesn't fit in with a regular school. I actually dropped out of high school art after the first year, because it was so suffocatingly structured, and the teacher was not even an artist herself.

Though one can train on their own and become a world-class and well-paid artist, it is much rarer to find these types in history. More typical biographies from artists in history include long periods working as illustrators for magazines or newspapers; training from childhood under a parent or under formal tutelage from a master artist; or training from childhood in a school which dealt exclusively with art. On top, most biographies contain years of production after their training before their sales make them a success.

Picasso was a rebellious artist, producing some of the wildest images of his time, but he still seems to have derived much of his career path from what he learned in art school. I am sure he learned some things about form and technique, but really, he learned about the art world, the market, the critics, the history, and so on.

He learned what his work would be compared against and he learned what tends to be favored in the market he was growing up in. Importantly, he entered a proper art school in Barcelona at the same age he would enter high school today. A few years later he was ready to begin his career in Paris. Not only was he confident in his brush strokes from all of the childhood practice and adolescent instruction, but by learning what the art world was all about, he had all the information he needed to subvert the expectations of that same art world. He created a monumental stir and buzz which has lasted over a hundred years so far. His brand is still marketable today.

Systems of apprenticeships and serious training academies are the norm in art history, which is just about the opposite of what we have today, with art nearly always being an unimportant and irregular activity we experience in school, with everyone getting a participation grade and a pat on the back because art is subjective and therefore everyone did a good job.

Since governments control education and do not prioritize art, we are not really taught art theory or practice. This is less true in Europe and Australia and some other countries, but generally the result of this absence in education is civilian populations completely ignorant of art. Modern western populations wouldn't even know *how* to support the arts, or how to judge or interpret it.

Is this ignorance the fault of the government? Yes. Governments created the school system which keeps us in their buildings for most of our growing years. Most of our parents did not have the option to homeschool or send us to a private or specialty art school. Over more than a hundred years they have reduced the arts to the shadow it is now. Artists are left to find their own inspiration and education about their trades. If governments did not force their generalized, standardized version of education, we would have more art and artists.

Consider how much of modern music is produced by rebellious artists. From rock and roll to hip hop, punk to pop, the dominance of a rebellious attitude is no surprise to me. You almost have to be a rebel to even be an artist if you grew up in the modern world. Our parents typically don't want us to aspire to painting or dancing or singing or acting. Of course there are famous and wealthy examples in each category, but this is seemingly more of a lottery than a viable career path.

In most western countries, your parents are considered criminals if they allow you to leave school "early." In Canada it is illegal for a child to drop out of school before age 16. If I wasn't forced to attend school in those crucial years, memorizing and repeating the quadratic equation, I might have been able to actually train in art. Most of the greatest artists of all time spent their early years in heavy study, apprenticeships, practice, and they never learned the quadratic equation.

The fact that governments own art is not good enough for me to say that their involvement is a good thing, and I do believe their sanitizing and favoring "politically correct" art is overall bad for everyone involved. In the end, rather than supporting unleashed art, we mostly get outdoor decorations, which can already be done by muralists and mostly for free, or statues, which tend to be very expensive for whichever purpose they serve.

Like most other things the government is in charge of, their art collections are mostly centralized and off limits to most people at most times. If you don't visit the major cities you will see no government art, and will probably receive no instruction or inspiration about art in the school you attend.

If I were in charge of government budgets, I would also have a hard time justifying investment in the arts. The benefits of making the collections more widely available are too vague to measure. The costs would be high, and the benefits would have to be accepted largely on faith. If there were to be specialty schools, and they would have to abandon standard curriculums.

I believe the government should have a very limited function. It has overstepped its role as middleman and has become the dominant influence on culture itself. This has been a disaster for culture and all of the arts that comprise it.

Though this subject is low on my list of qualms with the government, it is still close to my heart. I have attempted to operate as an artist in a society that is ignorant of art, and I am not surprised that there are so few thriving professional artists in our modern western societies.

To me, a larger and more powerful government means a smaller and more restricted art scene. I believe that the best art is art that comes from pure free expression. Governments do not generally support free expression or appreciate social or political criticism of the time or place of the artist, which is of course one of the primary subjects of art, literature, performance, and music.

We do not need governments to support art. If they were to support it, then in my opinion the very least that should be done is actual professional artists hired to teach regular flexible programs which offer real advice and criticism and broader context about the art world.

Governments can commission the best artists of today to produce things we can all enjoy, but so can every wealthy person or reasonably sized business. Artists today can make their living on social media, and there are many things we as a society and individuals could do to strengthen our art culture, but aside from funding formal training and exhibitions, governments are not a big part of this equation. I think more people should commission more art, but I do not think that this is an appropriate or necessary role for government to fulfill.

10. Police.

This could have been the first chapter, because it is definitely high on the list of objections that people would have to the idea of a world without government. Who would, or *could*, keep us safe?

Law is supposed to have two main functions, the first is prevention, and the second is punishment. We can examine them both.

When I was young, my friends and I committed various crimes every day. We broke things, we fought with other kids, sometimes we stole things, and a few of us sold drugs. It might sound strange to a civilian, but to us it was very obvious that the police *never prevented any crime we committed.*

In order for us to be successfully deterred from committing petty crimes, the prospective punishment would have to be *very* severe. Most crime is petty – murder and rape and serious property damage are a tiny fraction of crimes. Those who believe in law as a deterrent would probably have a hard time justifying serious jail time for children committing petty crimes. And people who believe that it is the primary job of the police to keep us safe, would simply be incorrect.

Police are usually only called for violent altercations if it becomes very serious. They are not really able to prevent these crimes – they show up to arrest perpetrators and do the requisite paperwork, but they do not really prevent these acts. It is more the *threat* of calling police that may act as a deterrent. Anyone who has ever filed a theft report knows that there is an excessively remote chance of the police finding your stolen bike – you probably have a better chance of finding it yourself.

<u>Type of property – Percentage Recovered</u>

Locally stolen motor vehicles – 56.1%
Miscellaneous – 12.9%
Firearms – 11.6%
Livestock – 10.9%
Consumable goods – 8.3%
Clothing and furs – 8.1%
Office equipment – 5.5%
Household goods – 4.4%
Televisions, radios, stereos, etc. – 4.3%
Jewelry and precious metals – 3.5%
Currency, notes, etc. - 2.6%
Total – 28.9%

Source: US Federal Bureau of Investigation, *Crime in the United States 2019*

The chart above clearly demonstrates that the police can do very little to help you in the case of most stolen property. Vehicles are the most likely stolen item to be recovered, and even then, there is only a 56.1% chance of recovery in America. There are no countries that are substantially better at recovering stolen property. Cash currency has the lowest chance of recovery, at 2.6%, and overall the rate of recovery for all stolen property is only 28.9%. The high rate of recovery for vehicles greatly distorts this picture, since most other categories are less than 10% recoverable.

The vast majority of the work of a modern police officer is simply to enforce the bureaucracy. They are there to oversee adherence to the endless rules we have about who can buy, sell, drive, build, and so on. The bulk of their working time is spent doing paperwork having to do with these bureaucratic crimes. Nothing to do with violence, or safety.

When real violence does happen, the regular police step aside for detectives and crime scene scientists to do their work. Both detectives and crime scene analysts can function privately.

The police are there to file the report about the stolen property, not to actually *find* the stolen property. They are there to write the report about the violence, not to prevent it. And much of what they do is simply to ensure that business owners and drivers pay the appropriate fees to the government.

As kids, sometimes we were caught for our petty crimes by our parents or police, but since we were young we usually avoided serious punishment. We would have to sit in our bedrooms for a while, and then we would be back out causing trouble. I really do believe in consequences, and we should have faced more of them, but only if they were very strong would we consider changing our behaviors.

Some of my friends were sent to military schools or juvenile detention centers to "smarten them up." Unanimously, this did not work. Each of my friends who were taken into the system were worse when they got out. Now in adulthood, they are still trouble makers. I have never met anyone who was successfully "scared straight" by a stint in jail, though I am sure that such people exist. Those who went into custody when they were young were usually willing to wear this punishment as a badge of honor – those who went to jail would have more respect on the streets than they did before.

Once in jail, one is put in the presence of many more criminals to learn from and compare notes. Of course, they all got caught and that is why they are there, but you will probably not find anyone in any jail who is there for their first offense – it might be the first time they were caught, but the chances are extremely slight that it was their first *crime*. Everyone I know who went to jail for any length of time, came out a bit smarter about crime.

It is easier to hide something than it is to try and find it, and it is much easier to commit a crime than to try and solve one. People go to school to learn detective skills, and the most sophisticated science we have in our society is deployed to aid criminal investigations – yet children can successfully commit crimes without any education.

I am not saying that crime is good, but I am saying that police are powerless to prevent *most* of it. Police cannot patrol everything all of the time, and even in a society with cameras everywhere, they cannot monitor them all – usually you would be caught *first*, and then they would search for and examine the footage.

I have been to places where police were on every corner and the punishment was extreme. In North Africa I witnessed police holding machetes stained burgundy with dried blood. Apparently the jails were already full of criminals, petty and otherwise, and so the common punishment was to remove a hand, foot, ear, or eye, right there on the street.

You would think that this extreme punishment would easily serve as a total deterrent to all crime, especially petty crimes. Who would risk stealing bread if it cost them an ear? Apparently the deterrent effect is still quite weak, given the amount of people I saw who were missing these extremities.

If police do not really prevent crimes, then all of their patrolling activities are a waste of tax money. How often do you think the police stop a crime in progress because they happen to be driving by? It is worse if these same police harass innocent people.

In my home province of Ontario, they have instituted desperately strong punishments for speeding. If you travel more than 50km over the speed limit, you currently face a fine between 2 and 10 thousand dollars, increased insurance rates, and up to 6 months in jail. A second offense is more severe, with up to 10 years in prison.

Interestingly, people are still regularly charged with speeding "50 over." Presumably some people were deterred, but all those who still speed were not deterred. How much stronger should or could the punishment be? How much cost is worth it to enforce this?

I have collected numerous traffic violations over the years, including speeding tickets, and yet I still speed. I do not do this recklessly to purposefully put myself or others in harm's way, and I bet that most speeders will also believe that they are not acting from malice.

Several of my friends have had their licenses taken away for some offense – usually drinking and driving. I really don't like alcohol and I do think it is highly irresponsible to drink and drive, but I am not willing to agree that severe punishments help the situation. In most cases, my friends just kept driving. Some of them have been caught numerous times and given more and more tickets or had their vehicles confiscated – yet they keep doing it.

Recidivism is the term used to describe rates of re-offense of a given crime. Most of the studies I have found from across the world declare that recidivism for impaired driving is around 15-30%. This means that approximately 15-30% of people caught for drunk driving will be caught again for drunk driving.

Recidivism rates are only able to tell us about cases which

were *caught* a second time. Since almost no one gets caught or punished for their first offense of any crime, we can also assume that recidivism rates for most crimes are significantly higher than what we are able to determine from police reports. This is because I assume the criminal will use extra caution after being caught the first time, and because it remains difficult for police to catch any criminals. Getting caught once does not increase likelihood of getting caught again – the dice are rolled fresh every time.

Recidivism rates for other crimes are much higher. The US Bureau of Justice Statistics in 2019 published a 9 year follow-up for arrest rates of previous offenders. For property crimes, drug offenses, and "public order" arrests, recidivism was over 80%. All violent crimes were in one category, and recidivism was over 70%. Sex offenses were over 60%. These data clearly show that anyone who commits a crime is very likely to commit another similar crime, regardless of the punishment. On top of that, recidivism rates were *highest* in the first year after the arrest, with a tapering likelihood in the years to follow.

How severe would the punishment really need to be to stop this behavior? As long as humans have control enough to drive their own cars, they will violate traffic rules, and as long as we continue to make more laws, we must have the ability to enforce them.

Some pundits might interject here that perhaps control should be taken away. Maybe this is a perfect argument for the removal of free travel, or freedom in general. We cannot speed if we're all forced to use self-driving cars, or are locked up. Removing freedom seems to be the only option left. In absence of total control, we will have a problem. My proposition is that freedom for everyone is much more valuable than the benefit we would get from subduing all possible violations.

Who benefits from these punishments? In my opinion, only

the state benefits. They get some tax money from the ordeal, and they get to continue to justify the jobs created to monitor our roads and behavior. The deterrent effect is apparently weak, and so the public and the driver is no safer than before when they get back on the road.

If we separate the two ostensible functions of police – prevention, and punishment – we can see that they hardly have anything in common. Having a sort of police as a response unit is much different from them patrolling – imagine ambulances patrolling, looking for accident victims.

Interestingly, crime in the modern world *has* declined, very significantly. I have included two excellent books in the *Recommended Reading* section at the end of this book to substantiate this point, and the following graph is true for practically any location on Earth you wish to research.

(Chart on following page)

Y axis = homicides per 100,000 people

Homicide rates across Western Europe, 1300-2016
Source: Eisner (2003) - *Long-term Historical Trends in Violent Crime*. In *Crime and Justice, 30, 83--142*

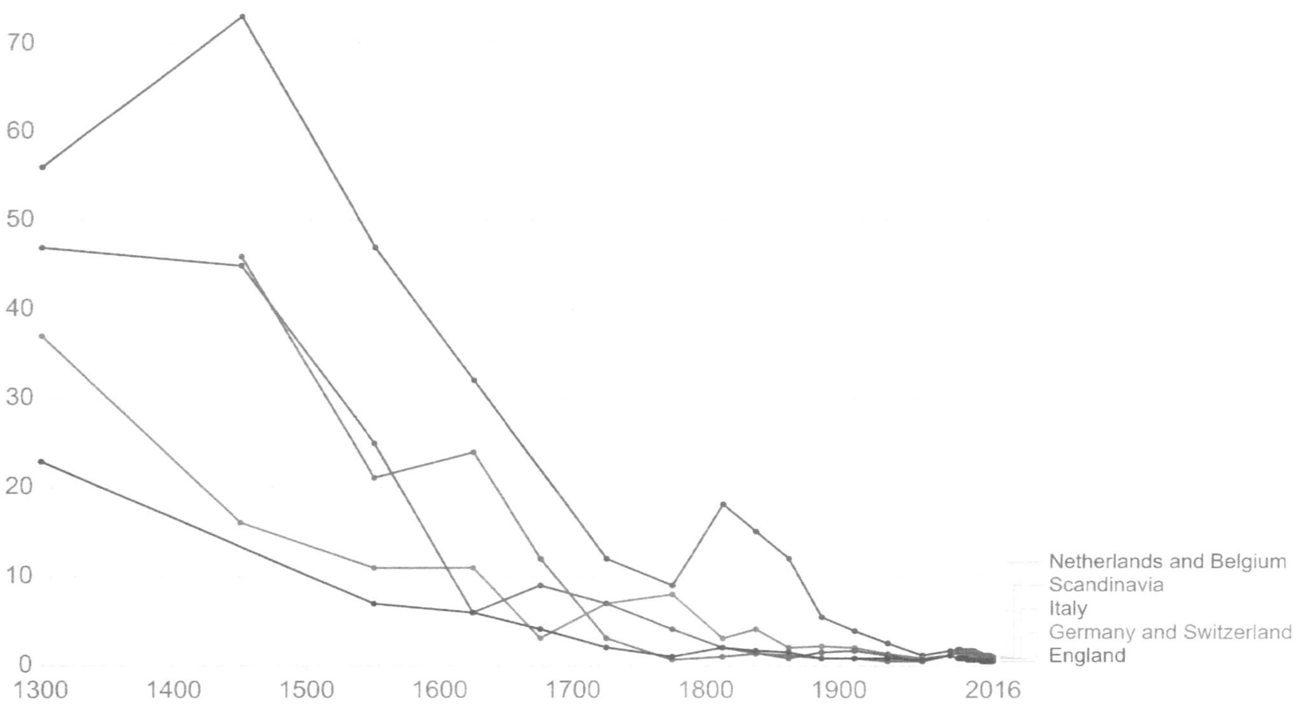

70
60
50
40
30
20
10
0
1300
1400
1500
1600
1700
1800
1900
2016
Netherlands and Belgium
Scandinavia
Italy
Germany and Switzerland
England

On top of the long-term decline in violent crimes in general across the world, in more recent years we have seen another impressive decline.

Reported violent crime rate in the United States from 1990 to 2019

Source: US Federal Bureau of Investigation, *Crime in the United States 2019.*

Reported violent crime rate per 100,000 population:

1990 – 729.6	2005 – 469
1991 – 758.2	2006 – 479.3
1992 – 757.7	2007 – 471.8
1993 – 747.1	2008 – 458.6
1994 – 713.6	2009 – 431.9
1995 – 684.5	2010 – 404.5
1996 – 636.6	2011 – 387.1
1997 – 611	2012 – 387.8
1998 – 567.6	2013 – 369.1
1999 – 523	2014 – 361.6
2000 – 506.5	2015 – 373.7
2001 – 504.5	2016 – 386.6
2002 – 494.4	2017 – 383.8
2003 – 475.8	2018 – 370.4
2004 – 463.2	2019 – 366.7

Many writers attribute this steady decline to the *presence* of government, but I disagree. I believe society itself is the best police. As we have become more prosperous and educated, crime has decreased, and peer pressure in communities and organizations keeps most bad behavior in check.

I would also argue that the introduction of the "smart" phone, and the accompanying cameras, have had one of the biggest impacts on crime in any period of history. We had already reached an unprecedented level of safety and security before everyone had a high definition video camera in their pocket, and now it is known by every criminal that they could be filmed doing anything inappropriate.

The civilian holding the phone is probably much braver in calling out the action than they would be without the phone. Obviously, this also gives every civilian the ability to report any crime instantaneously. Though the punishment itself is not a reliable deterrent, criminals will obviously aim to avoid capture, and thus the prevalence of phones gives them more incentive to pursue their activities off of the public streets.

This might not help much when it comes to sneaky break-ins and drug dealing, but it matters a lot when it comes to violent crime, especially outside of the home. When I was young we faced robbery every day on the street, and yet I haven't even heard of a public robbery in years. I am sure that altercations still happen, but the decrease is very noticeable, and crime statistics do prove that the trend is real. These days, you can probably feel safe walking through any inner city in America, and I attribute this to the phones.

Unfortunately, a lot of violent crime does happen inside the home. Police do almost nothing to prevent this. If they are called, they will take at least a few minutes to arrive, and many an angry father or husband has used this extra time to inflict extra pain and intimidation.

In Canada we do not have a "stand your ground" statute. So, if you defend yourself you may still be charged with assault or worse. This is supposed to decrease unnecessary violence, but what it really does is simply give more power to the state, and take power away from us.

I do understand the real threat of violence, even in our own homes. But I know intimately well from experience that the police can do almost nothing to prevent this. The best they can do is threaten us with more violence or judicial proceedings. As we have seen above, recidivism is very high in violent crimes, so the judicial system does very little to stem domestic violence, or violence between any two people who know each other.

I am pro self defense, and especially for gun ownership. In 1982 Kennesaw, Georgia enacted a local law which stated "every head of household residing in the city limits is required to maintain a firearm." The law was intended to deter crime, and it appears to be very effective. There have only been 3 murders in the town since the law was enacted, and that was almost 40 years ago at the time of this writing. Immediately after the law came into effect crimes against persons plummeted 74% compared to the previous year. Today they have a violent crime rate below 2%, which is among the lowest in any town in the world.

I should mention that the police in Kennesaw claim that they do not enforce this law. They do not come by your house to make sure you have a firearm. Yet the known prevalence of firearms in the town seems to be a remarkably strong deterrent for all violent, and property crimes. There are 4 other towns in America which mandate gun ownership, and they show the same trend of remarkably low crime rates.

We will likely never have a world completely free of drama, and violence is hardly the answer. But I do believe that if you are willing to stand up for yourself, your friends and community, that is one the strongest deterrents in existence.

There are other simple things that people do around the world to make their homes and properties safer. One is living together in communities and families. Another is having dogs, which are very effective alarm systems. Modern people have learned that even motion-triggered lights can reduce crime. South of the American border nearly every property has fences and bars on the windows. There are many ways to make things more difficult to steal and people more difficult to bully.

I eventually grew out of the criminal mentality, as did most of my young criminal friends. Young males are more likely to be violent, territorial, and to break any laws that are set down. But this is not necessarily permanent. Just as young boys are highly sexually motivated, it does not mean they will stay that way after maturity.

Young boys also comprise the majority of drug dealers.[x] Danger in general is mostly the territory of the young male.

Should we let young boys run amok and forgive everything they do? Hardly. There are solid deterrents in life, but these mostly have nothing to do with formal authority.

Any efforts at curtailing crime, with public or private money, should include things that give young boys something positive to do.

I have come to believe that we are most likely to be "bad" when we are "bored." As kids, we didn't have much to do other than cause trouble. It was a rush, it was much more fun than standing around, and we got to prove ourselves to each other. This could have been facilitated by something positive like sports or other structured, supervised activities. Authority and supervision are not the same thing, and I do believe we wouldn't have done such bad things if we spent our time in the presence, or at least the vicinity of adults.

For a brief time, we had a youth center in our neighborhood. Trouble makers of all ages hung out there, and to my memory there was not a single dramatic event – even though known enemies used the facility, nobody wanted to mess up the good thing we had there. We didn't want to hang out in the cold and this was the first time we had been able to congregate indoors *and* have actual activities there to keep us busy.

A heated facility with simple video and table games was enough to bring all the bad kids together and keep us largely away from trouble. In my adult life I have volunteered at a youth center and I do believe that this simple combination of positive activities and supervision is a magic cure for most troubled kids. The people who ran the center accepted us as we were, did not try to change us, and yet they ended up influencing us more than any parent or authority ever had. By the way, this was a private facility.

They say if you want to meet the devil, leave your schedule blank. Idle hands are largely a product of our prosperous society. Few peasants or farmers have the time or energy to indulge in real crime. Our wealth is good but our abundant "spare," unstructured time is, I believe, the cause of most addiction, violence, and crime in general.

As an adult I have learned to create a structured schedule, but there were years where I didn't have much to do, and I spent many days in depression, addiction, and criminality.

This idle hands concept leads me to believe that the government actually *produces* crime. How? Because you do not *have* to do anything in our type of society.

It is well established yet not well known that hunter gatherer societies are the most violent entities on earth. This point is counter to popular belief, but it is a fact. In the recommended reading section at the end of this book I have included resources to substantiate this very important phenomenon, and we will cover it further in the next chapter.

It is also well established that hunter gatherer societies have ample "free time." Men in particular have a lot of time to sit around and plan raids on other tribes. The result of this unstructured free time is a society with extremely high rates of violence. Rather than police punishing the criminals, it is most likely that the receiver of the previous violence will simply retaliate, and a cycle of violence is perpetuated.

Police would not stop this cycle – I believe it is only a busy schedule that will deter needless violence and most machoistic performances.

So, apparently the "rat race" has actually kept us out of a lot of trouble. And as we have continued to prosper in productivity, crime and violence have both steadily decreased. We are currently living in the safest time ever recorded in history.

Our prosperity has also allowed us to come up with systems of "social welfare." It is these systems I blame for much of the remaining crime and violence.

There are many cities in America and Canada, and other countries, which offer free money, free housing, and even free drugs to those who are "less fortunate." This is where the homeless people congregate. There are no "tent cities" in municipalities that do not support the homeless.

What about the slums of Nairobi, or Rio de Janeiro? One can read any random history book about Africa or South America and clearly see the result of hundreds of years of other governments producing what we now see as endemic poverty. I would argue that modern multi-government meddling in the form of International Monetary Fund and World Food Programme projects have further entrenched

122

this structural poverty.

This is why I do not support the recent "defund the police" movement in America. Notwithstanding conflicts of interest in the shady people and organizations who apparently fund the movement, (or the "black lives matter" movement), I do not think it is a good idea to defund the police in places that are essentially welfare states. When we have a welfare system that promotes degeneracy, we must also employ caretakers (police or security) to oversee the degenerates. This is why we currently have chaos in Minneapolis, Seattle, and Portland Oregon, and other cities which allowed their police forces to be defunded. It appears to be a bad idea to leave cities without police when those cities are full of people dependent on drugs and government programs.

Recently the *Wall Street Journal* published an article[2] about the immediate increase in crimes in the cities which "defunded" the police, and reported that most of these cities have reversed their decision, increasing funding in some cases beyond what they were before.

I spent a small part of my life as a drug addict, and I promise you that most of the people using welfare services are not "less fortunate." Find a greasy crack head on the streets of Denver or Los Angeles, and I will bet you they come from a decent middle-class family more often than not.

Drugs and alcohol offer everyone a great excuse to avoid action and responsibility. I believe the worst thing that governments have done to our cities is to provide "welfare", especially in the form of free drugs. Free money from the government does not provide anyone the incentive to do better in life. And when they pay you more when you have more children, the result is simply bigger families on welfare.

---

2 *Cities Reverse Defunding the Police Amid Rising Crime – WSJ* May 26, 2021

I should mention that I have received welfare, and I do not believe that I deserved it, or truly needed it. I was purposefully avoiding responsibility in my life, and the welfare only helped me prolong my commitment to becoming a responsible citizen.

Does this mean we abandon those who are actually in need, or those who are actually disabled? I believe we should all take more responsibility for those less fortunate. We should all extend a helping hand to those who need *and* deserve it. And we can support organizations that offer help to those who legitimately need it. I do believe some serious discrimination is wise here – rather than simply offering anyone the ability to suck the state's teat.

I do believe in charity, and it is perfectly reasonable to assume that private institutions and families can look after the few who really do need it.

The reality is that many or most homeless people are not on the street begging for change and standing in line for their free government drugs. Many homeless people are staying with friends and relatives and are working towards their independence. Some of them *are* using state or charity temporary lodging for the less fortunate. Many of them are simply down on their luck temporarily. Similarly, many disabled people are not using government facilities, they are being taken care of by loved ones.

There will always be people who do not get the best end of the stick in life. There is also no perfect system that takes care of everybody indefinitely without other social consequences. But I would argue strongly that government welfare is responsible for much of the remaining problems in society. Much crime and suffering has been eliminated by prosperity, and many of the remaining homeless drug addicts only exist because the state supports these people.

There are many sources we could use to illustrate the fact that drug users commit far more crime than non users. I will quote an old US Department of Justice report from 1994: "The evidence indicates that drug users are more likely than nonusers to commit crimes, that arrestees and inmates were often under the influence of a drug at the time they committed their offense, and that drug trafficking generates violence." These facts have not changed. These facts suggest that it is a bad idea to *support* drug users.

The reason for government supporting addictions is the strange belief that addiction is a "disease." Calling it a disease allows the "victim" *and* the society to believe that this affliction is not their fault. Having known addiction intimately, I promise that it is a choice – though I am not saying it is an easy choice, or that it is easy to get out of.

The drug user has put themselves in a difficult position by starting the habit, and it will take a ton of personal discipline and commitment to get out of it. Government welfare and free-drug programs make it very easy to stay stuck in the pit of addiction. This is clearly demonstrated by the fact that drug use, related deaths, and related petty and violent crimes, seem to be the only category of crime that has in certain places *increased* in recent years – despite the long-term decrease in crime across the board all over the world.

Addiction is reportedly increasing dramatically in America in recent years. The UN's World Drug Report in 2016 declared that heroin use had *tripled* since 2003. There is more awareness about the harm of drug use than any time in history, and yet the numbers suggest that this knowledge does not matter for dissuading use. I would argue that the increase in drug abuse is directly correlated to the increase in welfare spending.

According to the US Census Bureau *Annual Survey of State and Local Finances*, from 1977 to 2018, in 2018 inflation-adjusted dollars, state and local government spending on public welfare increased from \$143 billion to \$718 billion – a 402% increase. Over the same period, all other spending increased by roughly 150 %.

Welfare spending has been increasing, with no trend of reversal. The Urban Institute in 2021 estimates that 19% of the US population currently receives welfare. Some might argue that social assistance seems to have an opposite trend in countries like Denmark, and though my focus in on North America, I would argue that in Europe in general there is very much a concurrent drug problem, strongly correlated with welfare spending.

Government welfare takes responsibility away from the individual, and actually away from all of us. It is very difficult for us to help the addicts we know and love, because they can just go and get free government money and drugs if they don't like how things are under our care.

Governments classifying addiction as a disease has coincided with a decrease in penalizing addicts when they commit crimes. I have just made a case above that police are not very good at deterring, but having a system which punishes you *less* when you are a "victim of addiction," seems clearly to promote more bad behavior – they know they won't be punished.

While violence and crime generally continues to decrease throughout the modern world, we continue to fund (and increase funding for) welfare programs in locations of high drug use and high crime, and we have to deal with the resulting upsurge in crimes perpetrated by drug addicts and dealers in those areas. All of this, in my opinion, is caused by government welfare and liberal lenient punishment policies.

I seem to be calling for "more government" when I suggest that punishments for these people should be stronger, but I really would rather simply see the government stop supporting these people, and stop suppressing the rights of regular citizens to defend themselves and their property. Lenient punishment for "victims of addiction" is just a method of tacit support for their behavior.

The state of Oregon is a good example here, because in one way they used government legislation to reduce access to a key drug causing huge proportions of their crime, and in another way have used legislation to reduce consequences for crime now resulting from mostly other drugs. Oregon's methamphetamine epidemic was stemmed largely by making the base pharmaceutical ingredient harder to acquire[xi], but it has long been lenient on repeat offenders. Some addicts can see the same jail booking facility a hundred times or more. The leniency does not seem to do anything to stop the problem.

A jail sentence might not deter someone from using drugs, but at least it forces them to dry out for a while. It seems less expensive to society to lock them up for a time rather than have them commit crimes at will. It *is* expensive to lock anyone up, but I would argue that the violence perpetrated by drug users, particularly in the case of rape, is so egregious that it far outweighs the cost of prisons. Possibly the most insidious aspect of this lenient arrangement is that regular, law-abiding and sober people are helpless to take action against these dangerous drug addicts, because they will actually be persecuted with full force – since they are not a victim of addiction.

What is the solution here? We can at least stop funding the problem. Stop giving people free drugs and money and housing. Stop paying people more money to have more and more kids. We should feel that our life is our responsibility – not that we can fail in life and it doesn't matter because government welfare will take care of us.

I don't take any of this lightly, as I have had friends die from overdoses and I myself could have ended up a similar statistic. Most of the people I know who died from drugs were "taking advantage" of government "support." I feel very strongly that in a society which did not support such bad behaviors of drug addicts, those people would mostly still be alive, and maybe some of them would have actually contributed something to society.

Believe it or not, there are many places in the world where there are no police. I have lived in one of them, in the jungles of the Pacific side of Costa Rica. In our village there was a little outpost for police to come and process a criminal if a case did arise, but this is mostly just a formality, for there are no officers stationed in town and it would likely take at least a couple of days for them to show up if they were called – so they are not going to help you with a burglar or domestic disturbance. In any case, I never saw the building used.

There is still some crime in the area. In my time there, I know of at least one death in a bar fight, and some thefts – mostly cameras and other expensive equipment stolen from tourists. Would police stop this? Probably not, but I believe that prosperity would stop most of it, and I do not think it is possible or desirable to have a world in which no crime was *possible*.

Why would it not be desirable to have a world without the possibility of crime? Because this would mean either that we have absolutely no freedom, or that we have absolutely no property. Since people still break the rules in prisons, I assume that we would actually need to be tied down to *completely* ensure that no rules were broken. I imagine that we would have to be either sedated or under total domination to commit no crime at all.

I cannot envision any arrangement which completely alleviates the possibility of breaking the rules. Minimizing the rules themselves seems to be the best way to reduce the overall burden of trying to control people's behavior – after all, every rule must be enforced with the threat of force.

Despite the few crimes, some areas with zero police (and no welfare state) are remarkably safe from my perspective. Since you know that no police are coming, you also know that the homeowner or father of the girl will readily take action into their own hands. Locals do not mess with each other, and I have never witnessed a serious altercation other than that drunken brawl.

On top of that, addiction is practically non-existent, since there is no government to pay for it. In the village, there was one town drunk. I will call him Fred. Fred loved to drink, but without government support he had to either earn the money to buy drinks, or beg others to supply his habit.

No one in the village would support Fred's bad habit. They had absolutely no sympathy for him. The only people who would buy him the occasional drink were gullible tourists. Fred knew this, and so he spent a lot of time attempting to befriend any foreigners who happened to be in town. This worked sometimes, and he was able to get drunk off of their charity.

Most of the time, Fred had to work to earn enough money to get drunk. Sometimes he was sleeping on the concrete steps of the bar, and other times he was up early and captaining a fishing boat.

Fred does not live an optimal existence, but at least his terrible habit was not able to fully consume him, and he was not able to do much damage to anyone else. If he tried to steal from anyone in town, they would probably put him down like a bad dog.

Fred would occasionally run out of money, and that was a good thing. It would be awful if the government stepped in and "supported" him whenever he "needed" it. Fred also had family in town, and though they had been fed up with him for years, they would indeed lend a hand in times of dire need – but they wouldn't buy him a drink.

Officially, police and armies both exist to protect "the king's peace." We could be forgiven for thinking that they are there to "protect and serve" the public, but that is merely a slogan. Police work for the government, not for you.

Though I do not believe we need government police, I do believe in punishment, as long as we are not deluded into thinking that this has much to do with deterrent or "rehabilitation." Punishment could also mean *consequences*. There should be bad consequences for our bad behavior, and good consequences for good behavior. This is already normal human behavior – if we are rude to people, they will be rude to us, if we are kind, they will also be kind, most likely.

There are lines in human communities that should not be crossed, and there are some people who are determined to cross them, no matter the punishment. Locking someone away, at minimum, will ensure they cannot hurt another civilian in the public realm for the duration of their incarceration.

These people will probably not be deterred, and punishment will not stop the underlying problem. Keeping them in jail is the best we can do, short of something more extreme. Many types of social programs and education can reduce crime, and much of this has already happened, but this has nothing to do with police. I do not believe the government has to exist in order for jails or punishment to exist. Places without police readily take responsibility for punishing detractors.

The private prison system in America has been heavily denounced by liberal commentators. I do not believe that any institution should have incentive to lock more people up.

This is a last resort, and it can be handled privately, profitably, and with dignity for those incarcerated, if we choose to. This industry could have proper oversight from the public and does not need to work in tandem with the king's police.

One way to reduce the incentive for prisons to incarcerate ever more prisoners is for them to be paid on a *per facility* basis, rather than a *per prisoner* basis. When the institution, no matter who owns it, is paid more for each additional prisoner, their incentive will be to encourage more and longer incarceration. But if they are only paid a set rate for their entire facility, they are now incentivized to keep attendance in the facility to a minimum.

The most effective deterrent available is social pressure, in my opinion. In strong communities and groups this works fantastically well. It is those who fall outside of the community who are in most danger of not caring about the opinions of the community, and thus not being deterred by them. Police have nothing to do with this. We create our communities and it is our responsibility to be good friends and neighbors and to foster a strong cohesive society.

A strong supportive community does not mean that we give free drugs to anyone who wants it or free housing to anyone without a place to stay. Some people deserve help and others do not.

We are wrong if we think that punishment itself is a deterrent – it does not seem to be. But we do have a deep internal sense of justice, and I do not believe we will simply evolve out of that. We already know that people believe in justice, and this is the reason we don't go around knocking the hats off of strangers – they will probably take action against us, with or without police.

We can supply our own justice, as long as we are not prevented from doing so by the government. The state has monopolized the use of force in most modern places, and there are very few people who will agree that they always use this properly. It would have been too easy to fill this chapter with examples of police brutality, but of course this is one of the more popular grievances with modern police.

Allowing only the government to use force creates easy opportunity for the abuse of power – police brutality would not exist without police. State-enforced discrimination would also not be possible.

Courts and judges do not guarantee justice, and neither does vigilantism. But if I were to choose the freedom to pursue my own justice, or allowing the government to handle it, I trust myself much more.

There will probably never be total agreement about what constitutes "fair punishment," and so it does not matter whether the government or the people are in charge of it, because there will always be disagreement on how exactly we should handle those who harm others.

I am much more fearful of the guy on the street punching me in the face for something I did, than a cop coming to arrest me for it. The judgment and persecution of our peers and neighbors is a reliable deterrent for most bad behavior. We are likely to "tow the line" for our community to avoid informal punishment.

I believe we should be allowed to protect and defend ourselves. This, coupled with prosperity and productivity, is what will eliminate most crimes, in my opinion.

I haven't really mentioned police corruption, but this is also a clear possibility. It is also possible for, say, a private prison to be corrupt as well – for example, by allowing drugs to be smuggled in. It is probably impossible to completely ensure that all rules are followed.

But there are much more egregious cases of corruption that are definitely only possible by way of government policy. Operation "Fast and Furious" was said to be the "Watergate" of the Obama administration. This operation essentially involved guns being given freely to Mexican drug cartels. The government actually encouraged law-abiding gun store owners to participate in this mission.

The fact that they were giving free guns to violent gangs was not actually the scandal itself – the scandal was that they had lost track of the weapons!

This is only one example of a ridiculous operation conducted in the name of the long-standing and long-failed "war on drugs." The war on drugs has many pundits and I am one of them, but for our purposes here it is only worth mentioning that police can do much more than simply fail to keep us safe – they can quite easily make us much less safe when they pull crazy moves like this.

Though I am against state-funded police, I am in favor of private security.

I like to spray-paint buildings and bridges. Over the last 20 years I have been caught by police a few times, and they have let me go. Apparently, they did not want to be bothered with such a small crime, and they may actually get in trouble for processing us. Judges do not want to see petty cases, and nearly everyone in society seems to agree that it is not a wise use of tax dollars to lock up petty criminals.[xii]

Many times I have been looking to paint a place when I noticed private security check on the property. The risk/reward ratio was quickly shifted and I chose not to paint there. In other words, private security was an excellent deterrent.

If police checked around every old building in an industrial area, it would probably be a rather obvious waste of time.

They would be getting calls on the radio to go where people actually live or congregate, because that's where things tend to happen. As a response unit, it doesn't make sense to patrol in most places. We could have a private response unit. Neighborhoods have created all kinds of watch programs and those can be expanded with modern technologies, alarms, cameras, and lights.

I do not believe that "All Cops Are Bastards", as the slogan says. I know some cops who are, by my judgment, outstanding people. There are indeed men and women who want nothing more than to "protect and serve" the public. Private security would be an excellent career for these people.

Actually I do not believe it would be wise to fire the police or army, or bureaucrats for that matter. If we are aiming for a better world, it is hard to believe that campaigning against so many good jobs and ostensibly good people would be good for our campaign. I cannot envision any successful transition which does not have the support of the army and police.

Though I do not claim to have a perfect system or a roadmap to get there, I do believe that we can shift the way we make decisions, and reduce the responsibilities of the government, without harming the careers of the majority of the people working for the government. New hiring could be frozen, and remaining civil servants could be paid their salaries and agreed benefits as according to their original contracts. This would leave us with an army and a lot of equipment that could be put to useful work if we chose.

Police could be given less to do, less incentive to enforce bureaucratic crimes, and more personal discretion.

Police are under pressure to give tickets and make arrests. If crime goes down, police forces could theoretically be downsized. This is how we have come to have ticket "quotas" in some places, where officers have to hand out a certain amount of fines, essentially to justify their further employment. This seems to encourage *more* crime – things that might have been handled with a warning or a talk might be handled with formal prosecution simply because officers are incentivized to find more crime.

Security guards are paid to *make sure there is less crime.* They are not rewarded for handing out more tickets or arrests. If nothing at all happens on the properties they are in charge of, they have done a great job. They are not in fear of losing their jobs after a peaceful year.

Private security guards are much less likely to abuse their power, since they do not have much power. Their job is to help maintain basic order, and there are hardly any popular examples of security guards abusing anyone. If a private security guard abused their power, they would likely face public outrage – they are not backed up by the king, as they are not mandated to protect the king's peace. They are mandated to keep the peace of the property, or to manage a crowd, and their domain could be expanded to take on other current responsibilities of police.

There is only one type of world that has zero crime, zero violence, zero frustrations, dramas, or complaints – that is a world without humans.

Changing human behavior seems to be quite difficult. One easy way to reduce crime, is to reduce laws, rather then punishing people for their behavior and hoping they change.

I am from a place where it is illegal to be practically anywhere outside of a private property with any open alcohol. I have also seen countries where this is not a law, and even though I don't drink, I much preferred the atmosphere where people were enjoying themselves outside, rather than being confined into patios and bars and private parties.

When everyone is allowed to drink in public, everything does not simply become a party. There are just more people of all ages outside hanging out.

Homeless people and drug addicts already drink and use drugs outside, and this is part of the reason they tend to migrate towards the places that allow them to evade real jail time. But in most of these places, it is illegal for the average person to sip a beer off of a designated property. If the police stopped caring about public drinking, it wouldn't change the behavior of the people who are already the problem.

Many pundits of "the war on drugs" built the idea that we were making a bad situation worse by locking up drug users for possessing or using drugs. We needed too many police to do all of this, and it wasn't stopping the problem.

Despite the huge problem that drugs pose, I do agree that it doesn't make much sense to lock people up *only* for having or using small amounts of drugs. But this idea seems to have become a minimal punishment for most other small crimes as well, and this is the real problem.

We don't need to punish people for having or using drugs, but we can punish them for harming people or stealing or the short list of commonly agreed lines that should not be crossed.

In this chapter I have made it seem like the police are the ones doing the punishing, but this is not really the case. The legal system of courts, judges, lawyers, and jails, is what does the punishing. Courts both public and private are subject to all kinds of corruption, and I cannot claim to have a perfect system to ensure otherwise. But I am in favor of this system either way, and the principles of human rights during the proceedings, innocent until proven guilty and all of that, are great things for our society to maintain, with or without the political branch of government.

I am even in favor of lawyers. It is great to have a profession dedicated to prosecuting and protecting people and businesses. Presumably we will continue to have domestic disputes and contract disagreements and copywrite claims that will need to be handled in something resembling a civil court today.

We can have law without government, and we can have protection without police.

11. War.

One of the strongest arguments in favor of government is the defense of nations. Without government, who would protect us from invasion?

It is worth pointing out that the only entities we would likely be concerned about "invading" us are other governments. Governments are the only institutions who are capable of real war. Without governments, we would merely be left with human squabbles.

There was indeed war before civilization, though it was on a much smaller scale. Governments have not stopped war. But, just like violence, outright warfare has indeed decreased across the world. Deaths from violence of all causes are down to record lows, in terms of percentages of populations actually affected by conflict.

On the following pages I have shared the raw numbers for a graph showing the difference between violence in state societies and nonstate societies. I recommend Steven Pinker's *The Better Angels of Our Nature: Why Violence Has Declined*, and Lawrence Keeley's *War Before Civilization: The Myth of the Peaceful Savage* for further elaboration of this crucial point. The graph in the previous chapter showing the overall decline in violence over the centuries is also illustrative of this point.

<u>Rate of Violent Deaths in Nonstate and State Societies (Violent Deaths per 100,000 People per Year):</u>

Source: *Our World In Data*

Nonstate Societies:

Kato (Chato), 1840s (California) – 1450
Grand Valley Dani (New Guinea) – 1000
Piegan (North American Plains) – 1000
Dinka, 1928 (N.E. Africa) – 970
Fiji, 1860s (Melanesia) – 870
Chippewa, 1825-1832 (Minnesota) – 750
Telefolmin, 1939-1950 (New Guinea) – 740
Hewa (New Guinea) – 731
Buin (Salomon Is.) – 710
Mtetwa, 1806-1814 (S. Africa) – 590
Goilala (Papua New Guinea) – 550
Dugum Dani, 1961 (New Guinea) – 480
Manga, 1949-1956 (New Guinea) – 460
Modoc (California) – 450
Auyana, 1924-1949 (New Guinea) – 420
Gebusi (New Guinea) – 419
Murngin, 20 years (Australia) – 330
Tauade, 1900-1946 (New Guinea) – 320
Mae Enga, 1900-1950 (New Guinea) – 320
Yanomama, 1938-1958 (Brazil) – 290
Yurok (California) – 240
Mohave, 1840s (California/Arizona) – 230
Gebusi, 1942-1982 (New Guinea) – 200
Yanomama, 1970-1974 (Brazil) – 165.9
Tiwi, 1893-1903 (Australia) – 160
Boko Dani, 1937-1962 (New Guinea) – 140
Eskimos (central Canadian arctic) – 100
!Kung (Kalahari) (before state established) – 42
!Kung (Kalahari) (after state established) – 29
Andamanese (Indian Ocean) – 20

State Societies:

Mexican mestizo village, 1961-1965 – 251.2
Central Mexico, 1419-1519 (Mesoamerica) – 250
Germany, 1900-1990 – 160
Russia, 1900-1990 – 150

France, 1800-1899 – 70
Tepoztlan, Mexico, 1922-1955 – 59
Japan, 1900-1990 – 30
World, 20th century (wars & genocides) – 6
USA, 20th century (war deaths) – 3.79
World, 2007 (battle and one-sided violence deaths) – 0.33

As with crime, I attribute this decline largely to our increased prosperity and education. Educated and prosperous people seem to abhor violence.[xiii] Many of us will actually risk personal harm to stand up to our own governments when they are bullying other countries.

Just as I am in favor of the personal right to defend ourselves, I am in favor of armed populations, ready to defend their lands if necessary. And like private security, I am in favor of a private or voluntary defense force at the ready.

Most modern countries have not been invaded at all in modern times, and there is no obvious threat. I do not believe that our borders would be invaded the moment we decommissioned a government army. Would Canada invade America, or the other way around? What would either be looking to get out of the occupation?

Most of the so-called tyrannical governments of today are not really threatening invasion – Iran seems to want to be left alone, and North Korea is not attempting to invade either China, or South Korea. I see no reason why populations couldn't be prepared to defend their borders as they should be prepared to defend their homes.

There are exceptions. One of them is Israel, which is very openly interested in stealing land from bordering nations. Israel has invaded all of its neighbors, and is continuing to persecute and occupy Palestine to the point of genocide. All of the world's governments have stood by, and most of them continue to *support* Israel's aggression.

I would argue that Israel's strategy of invasion has only been possible *because* of governments. It has neither been deterred nor punished for its offensive.

There are some places on Earth that are still in disputes over land. The land surrounding Israel is one example, as are several areas of the Balkans. When you think about it though, who exactly is contesting what? To my knowledge, it is only governments disagreeing with other governments over borders. Israel greedily wants more land, and some governments want certain resources or more taxable subjects in their domain.

Israel is only able to persecute Palestine so morbidly for two reasons. The first is that Israel itself is extremely powerful. It is extremely powerful because it is supported by other governments. It is not private interests that give Israel the power to dominate its neighbors. The world support for the Israeli occupation is so strong that Palestine has been removed from maps all over the world.

The second reason is that Israel itself has prevented Palestine from gaining any power of their own.

Other governments have supported Israel, giving it more power, and other governments have participated in limiting the power of Palestine, leaving it easily dominated. The rest of the world has allowed Palestine to be starved of resources, which includes weapons. If they were armed and allowed to defend themselves, Israel would not be able to continue to bully them and steal their lands. This bullying is 100% facilitated by governments across the world – it is not the natural consequence of two peoples who disagree about borders.

Recently there was a conflict at the Armenian/Azerbaijani

border, though this is a much more even conflict than the total domination of Israel over Palestine.

I have avoided painting a perfect future strategy because I don't think that there is one. I don't think that the world will come to any agreements about dropping borders any time soon. In the last chapter I will make a case for a potential replacement for government, but my point here is that we can change the systems in our societies without having to change our borders.

We will probably always have slightly different ways of doing things in different places. Maybe some places strongly believe that they should provide welfare to drug addicts, where others strongly believe in punishing the users. This difference of opinion would be reflected in the rules of the territory, whether they are official "laws" enforced by a government, or customs enforced by a people.

The problem with war is that some governments have some extreme beliefs. Israel seems to believe that none of its neighbors have a right to sovereignty, and that the people who live in those neighboring countries do not deserve to live on that land.

The few conflicts in the world today are, in my opinion, only of two categories. The first is general racism, as in both the Israeli occupation of Palestine, and the Armenian conflicts. The second is domination by the largest power holders, as in the US occupation of many countries over the last century, or China and Tibet.

Most of the world does not fall into either of these categories. Canada has no ongoing conflict, no threats of invasion, and they are not threatening anyone either. Nothing would happen if we brought our troops home. Nothing would change except we would save a lot of money, and possibly gain some good will from discontinuing our presence in other countries.

It is too simple to say "we need governments to protect us from other governments." We must stop supporting government. If we stopped supporting the US government, it would have less power to support Israel, which would have less ability to persecute anyone. Tax dollars fund genocide.

Some have argued that there are genocides having nothing to do with governments, but I cannot agree. Situations such as in Rwanda in 1994 were created by governments in Uganda and Rwanda. The animosity between the two groups involved were fueled by these governments treating these two groups of people differently – the Hutu and Tutsi groups were not different races, they were different classes. There was not equality under the law and people from these different groups increased hostilities until violence erupted. Government is, as far as I can tell, always involved in major hostilities.

Similar conditions can be found in many countries in history, notably the Contras in Central America, where genocide was essentially funded by the US government to provoke political changes favorable to American interests. These situations were not merely people vs. people – they were people with the support of powerful governments vs. oppressed minorities or political dissidents.

Further, many such genocides occur while some rebel group aims to take control of the government. The structure of power itself attracted the violence. If there were no centralized power to take over, there would be no movement aiming to do so.

I am fine to concede a limited role to government. I would have very little to complain about if all they did was manage the contracts for roads and schools, or maintain a defense force. Governments have used the excuse of "protection" to launch offenses, and this will probably happen as long as we allow the government to be more powerful than we are.

There are a few countries who really do just want to defend themselves – Switzerland seems to be a good example. It is okay to have an armed and trained population, as long as we do not let our governments lie to us and tell us they are defending us when they are really attacking other countries.

Costa Rica has no army at all. Its neighbors are underdeveloped nations who could easily turn hostile. And nobody seems to be worried about an invasion. The Costa Rican people are just as capable of defending themselves as the people in the neighboring countries.

An argument could be made that no one is invading Costa Rica because they know that the US would come in and back them up. We could spin ourselves in circles with these arguments and come to no conclusion. I think it is clear that most modern, educated, and prosperous people have no interest in invading other countries.

It seems to me that the way forward is to encourage further education and prosperity across the world, regardless of any governments or lack thereof. I assume our trend of increased prosperity and education will continue, with or without government, as will our desire for peace.

One of the questions that came up as this book was being written was about human rights. Don't we need governments to protect human rights?

Here in the war chapter it is easy to argue that governments are the biggest cause of human rights violations. Governments oppress people and occupy territories. Governments prevented same-sex marriages and women from voting. Governments supported segregation and apartheid. And governments support other hostile governments or mercenaries which violate human rights when governments themselves do not want to be caught doing it.

Governments do not give us any rights. People all over the world believe that we have natural, God-given rights, and intuitive values about harming others. We believe that we have the right to personal sovereignty and should have the ability to vote and so on – it is governments who contest these rights, and we often have to fight the government in order to exercise our basic rights.

Finally, I have already mentioned my belief that nuclear weapons are a hoax, a lie perpetuated by governments. So I do not believe in "Mutually Assured Destruction." I believe one of the purposes of this MAD myth was to further justify larger governments with more secretive budgets that are focused heavily on weapons.

War is real, but I do not believe it is an active threat. To me, the threat is the government itself.

12. Services.

The government is in charge of only a few services in our society. One of them is mail – the postal service. This was a very valuable service earlier in human history, but now our economies and technological abilities are such that private entities are completely capable of handling this service.

"Government services" typically means the place where you go to get your drivers license or passport or to pay a fee in the town hall.

There are also very mixed results from government services. The US Postal Service is, in my opinion, one of the worst services in the whole world. They do a terrible job and they do it inefficiently and expensively. I am also endlessly frustrated by the Swedish Post (PostNord Sverige), or at least their customs department. I have had hassles with packages, and returned packages, from countries all over the world, and I often think to myself: "I really thought we'd have this figured out in the 21st century."

Apparently the atmosphere at the USPS has been so egregious that its employees have been prone to mental breakdowns. The phrase "going postal" was coined to describe the violent result of such disgruntled employees. Few of these people seem to have been upset because they were laid off. They did not go on a shooting spree because they lost their job – they snapped *because of their job.*

On the other hand, Canada Post, and Australia Post, are quite good – at least, the service is good. It is hard to credit the government with this, as the differences between the US and Canadian postal services are probably due mostly to their organizations and protocols, not the fact that they are funded by the government.

I was quite pleased to learn that Australia Post offered very reasonable rates for me to ship books overseas. This was great for me, but it really isn't necessary. A lot of tax dollars are used to float this service, and the discount on shipping books is not beneficial enough to outweigh the drain on the tax payer. Why should the Australian people pay for my books to be mailed?

Government funded postal services do not benefit any tax payer that does not use the service. I imagine that these days, in the era of electronic communication, few people use post other than business owners. So, the entire country pays for the benefit of private businesses and a few civilians.

I am very pro business, but I am against government supporting businesses. Capitalism should ensure that businesses are able to ship their products without government support, and this government support is not fair to the multitude of businesses who do not ship anything. We really do not need an elaborate tax system and army of bureaucrats just to allow us to have discounted shipping rates. This is basically a form of selective welfare for some businesses who use the service.

In any case, the discount is not that significant, as many private postal businesses are now very competitively priced.

My main problem with government services is that government employees are paid very well. I don't have a problem with people making good money, but I do have a problem with people making good money for jobs that do not deserve it. It is unjust that someone working for Canada Post will make more money than someone working for FedEx, for doing essentially the same job.

My local post office is very small, and there are only a few employees there. For the most part, these people are wonderful. They deserve a decent living. But the work they do does not necessarily justify their salary, insurance benefits, and retirement packages.

In my book *I Did It For The Money*, I argued that people should not be paid more for jobs that do not require much skill. The minimum wage should not be forced to increase by government meddling. There is a formula for building wealth, and it does not have much to do with the income you are paid. People can work unskilled jobs for a low wage and still build wealth, whereas they can also be paid very well and fail to build wealth. If they do not consciously employ spending and investment strategies aimed at growing wealth, they will likely be broke, no matter how much they earn.

Walmart is a private company that can pay its employees whatever it wants. As long as it meets minimum wage requirements, it does not have to pay a "living wage." But this is not true for government employees – they are expected to earn a living wage, regardless of the quality of their work.

Even a good service is not worth *that* much. Canada could offer free shipping to citizens and I would still not believe that it is a good use of tax dollars – again, not everyone needs or uses this service, so it is not fair for everyone to pay for it.

One of the employees at my local post office is a man I will call Dave. Dave is one of the most incompetent human be-ings I have ever met. He is a grown man and I honestly question how he made it this far. I question how he has not burned his own house down yet while making dinner.

Dave has screwed up several things in my presence. I make a clear effort to deal with someone else at the post office, as he is liable to do anything from messing up the label to hit-ting the wrong button on the computer. With Dave in charge, the simple package to my mother might be sent to Poland.

Since Dave works for the government, it is nearly impossi-ble to fire him – I guarantee that FedEx would have fired him. Government employees can be extremely incompetent and face no consequences. They can retain their employ-ment and retire happy. This is great for them and bad for us. Dave does not deserve his job, because he is terrible at it. Dave has no incentive to do a better job, because he is a government employee. The entire chain of command in the post office seems uninterested in overall performance. This is, of course, the opposite case of a regular business cli-mate.

We do not need governments to oversee any services. The ones they do claim responsibility for, they either do a bad job or provide the same quality service that a private busi-ness could.

Some people have told me that they feel their government provides a valuable service in the form of a public media station. In Ontario I grew up watching TVO – TVOntario. This is a government-funded channel, and I always appre-ciated the educational programming and the lack of explicit advertising.

But, I was always struck by the station's perpetual need for more donations. They were always asking the public for more money – yet they were ostensibly already funded by the public. This seems to be true with all public media stations in the countries I am familiar with. The government just can't seem to budget them properly.

Proper media production is expensive. The equipment is expensive, as are the many professionals required to operate the station. This is not a low-overhead venture, and yet private media companies are some of the most profitable businesses in the world. We are supposed to be grateful for a commercial-free content experience as a trade-off for public funding, yet this seems to inevitably fall short of what these stations actually require to operate.

I have never watched American public TV, but I have thoroughly enjoyed much of the programming on public channels in Canada and Australia. I have also felt uneasy about the government giving me information directly. Governments have terrible track records with selective information and propaganda, though I do believe that management has kept a fair balance on TVO at least – they are often very critical of government policies.

I just do not believe that this operation needs to be funded by taxes. I, for one, would happily donate to TVO if it were not already funded by the government. I enjoy the programming enough to support it, even on a subscription basis. I am sure many others would do the same, and this would provide a budget for the channel. I would also be fine with the channel seeking advertisement revenue. Every other type of media channel uses advertising as a primary income source. If a channel cannot garner sufficient revenue to remain in operation, then this seems to suggest that it should not be in business – this is capitalism.

Capitalist channels do not inherently invite corruption any more than public channels do. Every channel must decide on what type of content they will provide, and every organization will have its own biases that will show up in the programming. It is up to us consumers to decide what to watch, what to support, and this will determine which channels stay in business.[xiv]

Both public and private media stations tend to parrot whatever the mainstream opinion is. Both censor information, and this is the right of any media company to do – I also choose favored information on my own channels. There is nothing about a channel being public that makes it any more unbiased, or have any specific improvement on quality of programming.

Alternative views are invariably presented only on a minority of channels, which are typically private and independent of a larger media corporation – though alternative views do sometimes appear on public media, as well as conglomerate media.

One of the last comments I got on this manuscript was about airports. Don't governments ensure safe air travel?

After September 11th, 2001, governments created new departments to oversee unprecedented new security measures in airports. I do not believe this made us any safer, but I do believe it created many new jobs – unskilled, decent-paying jobs that one apparently does not need any basic human skills, manners, or respect in order to get paid.

Many government departments, including the Transportation Security Administration, seem to have absolutely no regard for human dignity. But they are for our safety, right? I would really like to know how. I would really like to understand how we are safer as a country when only one mode of transportation is guarded so heavily. Terrorists could strike in any crowded public space, and this nonsense about maximum fluid container sizes and no corkscrews does nothing to protect us. All it does is make the TSA workers feel important, and make our travel a lot more expensive, uncomfortable, and time consuming.

If we were actually serious about protecting each other, we would implement similar security checks on all public transportation, and anywhere that large crowds can gather. This would be terrible. The only absolutely safe world is one where humans have absolutely no power or control.

Of course no one is proposing total security, and that is exactly why government intervention in air travel has nothing to do with safety. If it was really about safety we would see these measures everywhere. It was not the airlines who decided to become so strict at airports, it was the government. They could have imposed into subway stations and shopping malls as well, but they didn't because they are only interested in creating jobs and the illusion of safety.

I personally believe that 9/11 was not perpetrated by cave men armed with box cutters, which is still the official government theory. I believe it was likely an elaborate hoax perpetrated by the American government. But even if the terror was real, it makes no sense to protect one mode of transportation and not the others.

I have attempted to avoid conspiracy theories in this book, though if any of them are true it certainly supports my thesis. Either way, security measures that do not protect us are indeed bad for us. False security is bad, wasting money is bad, and allowing government to take control of any part of our economy is bad for us.

I cannot think of any service that must be provided by a government, or that a government does a better job of than a private company. On top of that, even if they do a good job we have no way to ensure that the service is provided for a reasonable price. Governments do not seem to care how much it costs to operate their services, since it is our money paying for it.

They also tend not to care much about how their service is perceived, unlike a regular business that would try to be nice to you to keep your business – there is only one place to get your driver's license, so it doesn't matter how you are treated there.

The only exception here that I can think of is fire fighting. The problem is, many fire departments have proven success on a mostly voluntary system.

Firefighting is one of the most noble professions available, and you will not find anyone saying that fire departments are a bad thing.

Firefighting is a very efficient service. Firefighters do not patrol the streets looking for fires, but they show up when one is happening. Fire stations are very cheap to maintain compared to a hospital or police station, and fire equipment is durable and does not need frequent replacement.

We will always need fire fighters and we will always have them, regardless of government. People will always volunteer for the greater good, and the fire department will always be one of the first places for these people to exercise their humanitarian urges.

If the government did not pay for fire trucks and hydrants, who would? This is a great lead into the final chapter.

13. Our Only Option?

Despite my affinity for the anarchist philosophy, I do not believe it is appropriate to compare the small-scale anarchist societies to our modern world. Community values can run a community, but I do not think they can run a country, at least not any time soon.

Anarchists will go as far as to say that we should not even have borders or nations. I would agree in theory, but not as a practical starting point.

Everything the government does is bad for us, but it does not have to be this way. I think there are three separate aspects of government function that we should examine to see what can be done about the overall problem. These three aspects are *democracy*, *administration*, and *taxes*.

Democracy is touted as a wonderful thing, yet I see it as a mere justification for the existence of government. The idea of democracy is to elect "representatives" to speak for the people and make decisions on their behalf. Since we elect these representatives, this is said to be the most "free" and "fair" system of governance – opposed to communism, where largely unelected officials make decisions for everyone.

Democracy is a bad thing when we essentially have a decision-making class, disconnected from the population at large, and especially when these decision makers are not held accountable for their actions. Politicians are like celebrities, sheltered from the realities of the world, held up on a high horse of enlightened self-satisfaction, and too often they act against our interests and are usually not punished in any way.

There are some excellent politicians who deeply care about the wellbeing of the people *and* have a powerful understanding of how the world works. The problem with democracy is that anyone can be elected. Since anyone can be elected, it is not a necessity that they care or know about what might be best for the people – it is only necessary that they are voted in.

Campaigns can be very misleading, to put it mildly, and corporate dollars can buy exposure for anyone to be put in the spotlight during election times.

Before the age of easy communication that we currently live in, democracy was our best available system. It was totally impractical to attempt to organize the opinions of entire populations other than by simplifying the voting pool to those who have been elected as representatives.

Before this age of communication, the population also did not have access to the information they would need to make informed decisions. The concentration of information correlated with the concentration of power.

These challenges no longer exist, and so representative democracy is no longer necessary. Actually, I would argue that since public opinion is so easily manipulated in the media, democracy is now actually bad for us. We are nearly guaranteed to elect corrupt officials, since our exposure to those running for office is largely determined by how much media time they can afford.

With the internet, we now have the ability to access nearly all of the information in the world. We no longer need an educated elite to trust for wisdom. With the internet, we also now have the ability to speak for ourselves – it is now practical to bypass the representatives.

It would be very easy to create an official system of "direct democracy" - digitally. "Digital democracy" would give each of us the ability to vote on local, regional, and national matters. We could call this system "government", or some other name – the language is not as important as the change.

Those politicians who really do care about the wellbeing of the people will always be able to act as *influencers*. I believe that influencers will be the politicians of the future.

I am not convinced that direct democracy is actually the best system, though I do think it is better than what we have now. At least we could say we had a chance to vote on important things like wars and budgets. But, democracy would work best in a population that is highly educated on what they are voting on, and we are not quite there yet.

Businesses are run as dictatorships, and I believe this is for the best. Businesses seem to function very well when all members are able to communicate with the decision makers and offer opinions on improvements, but ultimately the majority of decisions are made by autocratic rule, not vote.

Often it is quite clear what the population wants. An example is the legalization of marijuana. In Canada, the last federal election that I participated in was won, in my opinion, on this single issue. Justin Trudeau vowed to legalize marijuana, and the population voted for him. I am ashamed to admit that I even voted for him, because of this one issue.

The problem with this is that there is more than one issue in this country. Legalization was one thing we felt strongly about, and we had to accept the rest of Justin's opinions as a byproduct. This has turned out to be a disaster, since this man seems to be keen on implementing a full-scale communist-type system of government control and "universal basic income."

The legalization scheme seems really to only have benefited the government, simply providing more tax dollars for a product that was formally "underground."

I for one did not really want legalization. When I was young we had an experimental period of "decriminalization", and that seemed to be excellent. We were allowed to use the already-popular herb without fear of being arrested. Legalization is much more about government *controlling* the substance, and taxing it.

We did not have an option to vote for decriminalization, even though the earlier experiment seemed to be quite successful. Since the only two choices we were given were between legalization and continued criminalization, we chose to legalize.

We are pigeonholed into limited options because of this system of representative democracy. Even worse, politicians can lie. Justin clearly lied about many hidden agendas, and he is definitely not the only politician to get elected with promises of candy, yet slip in insidious policies as soon as they get elected.

We can bypass the representatives by directly voting on individual issues. That way we do not have to elect people based on a few matching opinions, as in the case of agreeing with Justin about marijuana but disagreeing about most other things.

The next major part of government, *administration*, can now be handled in a very straightforward way. It would not be hard to administer the decisions made by this digital democracy. This administration could be facilitated by a private company, or by something resembling the public government we know now. The difference would be that instead of a president or mayor making decisions, they would only be able to act on the will of the people.

There would still be tough decisions and compromises to make, but the people making them could be held to a standard of transparency and accountability, and have less power to make destructive decisions overall. Politicians really could serve the people in this model.

Perhaps the basic structure of administration remains the same, yet the people vote overwhelmingly to halt all secret ("black budget") projects. Maybe they vote to bring home the troops, increase funding for schools and decrease it for government-funded cancer research. To me, this is a much better world already.

There are complications here that will never be fully settled. Anarchists and conspiracy theorists like myself will always be hesitant of any ID systems, and presumably we would need something similar to our birth certificate system to officially register for the digital democracy. I cannot alleviate every concern, but I will say that I am personally willing to concede a small bit of my ideals in order to see major progress made.

We might be most free in a world with no formal IDs at all, but I do not see that happening. We already have ID numbers from our birth certificate, or social insurance number in Canada or social security number in the US, and this could be used to ensure that you really do only vote as one person.

The digital democracy might resemble Facebook, and there will indeed be concerns about security and tampering, but I do believe that these are primarily engineering problems and are all solvable in principle.

Could a private company handle our administration? I think so. If the role of government really was just to middleman our desires and our tax dollars, I would readily accept a fee for a company to handle this. This company would be transparent by decree – we would ensure that they were transparent or we would vote to put the responsibility in the hands of another organization.

Neither private nor public government guarantees integrity – we the people must monitor our administrators constantly to ensure that they act in our interests.

Maybe a private government, like a private company, would actually attempt to *save* money, rather than spend every possible tax dollar in earnest. Maybe they would actually care about our national debt, rather than simply continuing to dig us further into debt. This brings us to the last major part of government, taxes.

It is commonly said by people like me that "all taxation is theft." I would agree insofar as we did not all agree to pay taxes. I was born into a world where I was never given an option on which taxes to pay. The best I was ever given was the option to vote for one of a few "representatives" who typically have only marginally different opinions about taxes.

I would agree to property taxes if these taxes paid for my local fire department, roads, and the other major necessities. I will never want my tax dollars to pay for any army or police, and I will never want my tax dollars to pay for a lavish dinner party for Chairman Trudeau.

Perhaps the direct democracy would give you the option of how much taxes you would like to pay and for what. Would everyone choose to pay nothing? I really doubt it.

All businesses tax their customers, and I am not talking about sales tax. If I buy something for 1$ and sell it to you for 2$, the extra dollar is the tax you pay for my service. This tax pays for the store or the salaries or whatever else is necessary for me to make the product or service available to you.

I would be in favor of a pay-to-use system. Private schools have you pay for tuition only when you have a child in the school – taxes have us all pay for every school forever, regardless of whether we ever use the service or not, or whether or not you are happy to be paying for small children to be learning about things you disagree with. You pay a lot during the time you use the service, and none otherwise.

As argued in this book, I would not have much of a problem if we were actually paying for good schools, but I do not want to pay for our current school system which is essentially expensive daycare that brainwashes the children.

A pay-to-use system might not work for things like firefighting. Those of us who never had a fire would be fine, but a system which charged the actual amount for the actual service might leave you with an unpayable bill for the fire department. This is why I would be willing to concede a basic, voluntary tax system that did pay for the absolute necessities.

I am not a fan of insurance, but perhaps an insurance program would alleviate the high cost of potential fire bills or medical emergencies.

To those opposed to the idea of a voluntary tax system, consider the idea that those who know the current system are already able to essentially choose how much tax they would like to pay. The easiest way to reduce the taxes you pay is to register a business. All wealthy people already divert their income into businesses, charities and charitable donations, and many of them move money out of their countries to "tax-sheltered" jurisdictions.

Wealthy people *already* choose not to pay many taxes. They pay the minimum. I am sure we would all like to pay the minimum. It is only by our ignorance that the common people pay more taxes than the wealthy. This doesn't sound very fair, and it isn't. It would be more fair if we had basic taxes on things like property or services, and much of the rest of the tax system was simply abolished. We wouldn't need tax havens if we had a fair and sensible tax system.

As pro business as I am, I do not believe that we should have so many options to manipulate our tax bills. One of the ways to do this would be to abolish income tax. Income tax in America was instituted in 1861 to pay for the civil war. Many countries also used the cost of a war to justify taxing their citizens, and other countries just followed the trend and implemented the cash grab without justification.

It seems that there are very few temporary taxes, just as there seems to very few temporary laws. All of the new laws and taxes created in the wake of 9/11 are still in place, and this is a large part of my current objection to all of the new taxes and fees being foisted on us in the name of the virus that governments shut down the world for. I do not believe that these new laws or taxes are justified, for one, but worse is the very reasonable assumption that once instituted, these new taxes and expectations will never go away.

There are some countries that have no income tax at all: the United Arab Emirates, Monaco, Bermuda, and the Bahamas. These countries operate just fine without income tax. There is no country that operates without any taxes, but income tax does not seem to be a necessary income for any government.

One might argue that these countries have such strong revenue sources that income tax is not necessary. This argument holds some weight when speaking of the UAE or Monaco, but Bermuda and the Bahamas are hardly economic powerhouses. The simple fact is that regardless of GDP, income tax is a cash grab perpetrated by governments onto their citizens.

America currently has 9 states without income tax: Alaska, Florida, Nevada, New Hampshire, South Dakota, Tennessee, Texas, Washington, and Wyoming. You will find more differences than commonalities between the economies of these states. The only major commonality is that these places choose not to gouge their citizens with extra, unnecessary taxes.

In addition to no income taxes, most of those 9 states also show up on the list of lowest business taxes in the country. So, a lack of income tax does not translate into a need to increase taxes elsewhere. It is not necessary because income tax was never necessary to pay for government – ostensibly, income tax exists to pay for war.

Even worse than a baseline income tax is "progressive" income tax – higher taxes for higher earners. This system is touted as "fair" by liberal thinkers, but I think it only creates incentive for those who make more money to move their money around.

If I am facing more taxes when I make more money, I will definitely attempt to *lower my taxable income*, by diverting funds into a business (which I can then "write off"), or by donating to "tax-deductible" charitable causes, purchasing art (often tax-deductible in many countries), or moving my money to a bank in a tax protected country. Some people even move to another country or state to lower their income tax.

Those who understand these tactics know very well that progressive taxes are just an illusion of fairness. I can simply buy art or give my money to my own charity, or to a property in another country, and avoid the tax. Progressive income taxes end up simply gouging the middle class more than they already are. Poor people already don't pay much tax, and rich people are adept at avoiding taxes.

There are only a few options here to improve fairness in this system. One would be to charge everyone the same percentage, regardless of total income. Another option would be to eliminate current tax deductions and punish all tax avoiders equally. And of course, a clear option is to abolish the income tax entirely.

This limited government that I propose might resemble the "libertarian" ideal, and though it is not pure freedom, it would be the closest that the modern world has ever seen.

I do not know how we would enact such major structural changes to our system of government. I do not believe that most of our elected representatives care what the masses actually think, and I do not think that they will willingly allow their institutions to change in any major way. If we collated our opinions into a digital democracy without their consent, I doubt they would pay any attention to it. I do not know how a replacement would take place.

I feel it is our duty to stop funding the government. One of the immediate things that every person can do to take tax money – and thus, power – away from governments is to register your own business. Even if you have a job, you can route much of your income through your business and reduce the total taxes that you pay. Speak with a qualified accountant to discuss your options.

There are two major aspects of our lives that we must gain control of in order to take power away from governments. The first is our health. It is completely within our power to achieve and maintain good health, and this immediately removes us from government healthcare.

The second is money. It is our duty to accumulate wealth so as not to be dependent on the system. As long as we are poor in health and in wallet, we are subservient to the government.

Personal health and financial health are both within our control, if we choose. I have written other books on these subjects which you can find in the *More* section of this book.

For now, I believe it is our duty to rebel against the government, as well as participate in the better world that we want to see. It is our duty to avoid all unnecessary taxes, licenses, and infringements upon our dignity.

We are far from a strong, informed, and empowered population ready to take control of our society, but those of us who do not like the way things are must be committed to promoting our ideas and pursuing any possible better options. The first step is simply to understand that *everything the government does is bad for us.*

More

I have a podcast, *Notus & Friends*.

@RyanAleckszander is my personal Instagram account, where I post mostly book reviews. My personal YouTube channel is *TheRealNotus*, where I post mostly my opinion, as well as read-along versions of my books.

@TranscendTowers is my cellphone tower Instagram account, as well as miscellaneous conspiracy material.

@TheRealNotus is my art Instagram account. I also have a YouTube channel *Notus Art*, teaching art on a budget. I have art for sale at www.NotusArt.com

@WallachsWarriors is our health Instagram account. We regularly answer live audience questions and we will answer every message in the inbox.

Our products can be found at:
www.WallachsWarriors.ca

@NotusFoods is our food Instagram account. We have talented cooks and bakers who will take requests and answer questions. We also have a YouTube channel *Notus Foods* to teach cooking according to our guidelines.

Our cookbook teaches everything you would need to know to cook without the bad foods on Dr. Wallach's list.

Dr Wallach's Cooking Without The Bad Foods

by Chef Norman Goodies | Jun 14, 2021

★★★★★ ⌄ 1

Paperback

$29.99

I have written a book about "alternative health" from my perspective in the business:

Fake Diseases

by Ryan Aleckszander

Paperback
$9⁹⁹

I have published a book in defense of Dr. Wallach, in response to his critics:

Nutri-smart rebuttal: in
defence of Dr. Wallach
by Ryan Aleckszander

Paperback
$9⁹⁹

I Did It For The Money is about my financial story and opinions about money and wealth.

I Did It For The Money

by Ryan Aleckszander

Paperback

$7⁹⁹

There is an extended version which also includes The Richest Man in Babylon, by George Clason. This version is available on Amazon Canada and Japan. Check the product description to make sure it is the longer version.

As well as any of the accounts above, you can email any inquiries to YGYOntario@gmail.com

All of my books and links can be found at:
www.NotusBooks.org

Recommended Reading:

This list could have been a lot longer, but these are some books that cover ideas referenced in the text.

- *Wheat Belly* – William Davis

This is an excellent account of the history of wheat. Understanding this food is all you need to know to agree that governments should not be subsidizing it.

- *Nutrition & Physical Degeneration* – Weston Price

This is one of the most important historical texts about natural nutrition. Understanding how primitive populations were able to remain healthy is an excellent comparison to modern government-funded healthcare.

- *Food INC.* – Karl Weber

The food industry would not exist as it does if it were not for their strong relationships with government.

- *The Case Against Fluoride* – Paul Connett

This is the whole story of how governments colluded with industry to add toxic industrial waste into public water supplies.

- *Everybody is Sick and I know Why* – Peter Glidden

Truly understand the absolute failure of modern medicine, and how they attained this monopoly through cooperation with the government.

- *Dissolving Illusions: Disease, Vaccines, and the Forgotten History* – Suzanne Humphries

Governments seem to love vaccines. I believe they are a complete scam at best, and murder at worst. The eradication of infectious disease was due mostly to hygiene. Humphries details this argument exquisitely.

- *The Skeptical Environmentalist* – Bjorn Lomborg

There are many environmental myths that are still promoted by government agencies. We should understand how to examine environmental data critically.

- *Endgame: The Hidden Agenda 21* – Vernon Coleman

This is the clearest examination of the one world government currently being implemented under the guise of "sustainable development".

- *Drive: The Surprising Truth About What Motivates Us* – Daniel Pink

This book summarizes the various theories of human motivation and makes a strong case that what really brings out the most productive and fulfilling work from human beings are essentially the exact opposite of how we are taught in modern schools.

- *Debt: The First 5000 Years* – David Graeber

Our relationship with debt is probably the least understood but most important part of our existence in society. Government involvement with our money system has a long and nefarious history.

- *The Utopia of Rules* – David Graeber

Though this book is a bit off topic pertaining directly to the government, it does go into brilliant detail on the many use-less functions of government bureaucracy, and police enforce-ment of the endless rules generated by our bureaucratic sys-tem.

- *The Better Angels of Our Nature: Why Violence Has Declined* – Steven Pinker

This book goes into great detail on the decline of violence and the myth of the peaceful savage.

- *War Before Civilization: The Myth of the Peaceful Savage* – Lawrence Keeley

This book further elaborates the point that we are more peace-ful now than we ever have been.

- *Confessions of an Economic Hitman* – John Perkins

Government practices can be much more insidious than we have covered here in this book. John's story is incredibly eye--opening.

- *With Liberty and Justice for Some: How the Law Is Used to Destroy Equality and Protect the Powerful* – Glenn Greenwald

Greenwald makes an excellent case that the principle of equal-ity before the law has been eroded in modern times, to the point where there are at least two separate systems of justice – one for the common people, and one for an elite group who is essentially empowered to break the law at will. This is an clear demonstration of government favoritism and power harming the very fabric of our society.

- *The 9/11 Commission Report: Omissions and Distor-tions* – David Ray Griffith

I didn't really get into 9/11 in the book but it is a great example of the possibility of governments to do great harm to their citizens – to put it mildly. Griffith goes into painstaking detail to prove, undoubtedly, that at the very least the American government has lied to its people and the world about one of the most destructive single events in modern history. Whether you believe that it was an "inside job" or not, this excellent work makes it clear that the government is prepared to lie about the basic facts. In either case, this is a clear example of Bad Government.

On a similar subject, I made a full-length documentary film about the history of "false flag" operations. In that video I purposefully excluded 9/11 because I thought it was low-hanging fruit – all of the conspiracy world already knows about 9/11, so I focused on dozens of other incidents that appear to be false flag operations coordinated by our government with the aim of further restricting our freedoms and perpetuating a system of total control over our lives.

This video, of course, was banned on YouTube and Bitchute. I have created a website to host the video, www.WagTheDogTheory.com, where you can view the uncut version for free. I recommend downloading it if it is still up.

In that documentary I use video evidence to suggest that the entire 2020 pandemic event was itself a staged false flag operation. This is a big claim, but if any of these events really were perpetrated by our government, this is one of the strongest arguments I can think of to support the thesis of this book.

Alphabetical Index

i   It is worth noting that in addition to the federal or state gas tax, that total is then taxed with a sales tax, which in Michigan is not spent on roads. Instead, nearly three-quarters of sales tax revenue collected on fuel sales goes to the state's School Aid Fund, with the rest split among local revenue sharing, public transit and the state's discretionary general fund. – *Bridge Michigan*, Feb 11 2019

ii   This information is from www.Ontario.ca.

iii   The flip side of this "book price" concept is perhaps not as egregious as having your land forced from you at a non-negotiable price, but it is odious nonetheless. Once I was given a beat-up old pickup truck for free that we affectionately called Old Blue. To have this vehicle legally on the road, I had to pay taxes on the sale price. The sale price was zero, but of course the government of Ontario does not care what the bill of sale says.

The "market value" of that truck was apparently over $6000. It did not matter that Old Blue had been worked into retirement, and that the taxes I was being asked to pay were easily more than the whole vehicle was worth.

Old Blue now lives on my friend's property, as even though it is technically legal, it is not roadworthy. That property was nothing but trees when my friend bought it, and the taxes were very low. We built a single-room wooden cabin, which was more like a shed and did not have a "proper" foundation – it lives atop cinder blocks. The act of building this shed immediately increased the "book price" of the property, and the property taxes consequently doubled. But I digress.

iv   For instance, Florida's Lake Okeechobee Dike is protected by the Army Corp. of Engineers. It's a public trust. They say that communities own the borders of Lake Okeechobee, but in reality the government controls the lake under jurisdiction of the Army Corp of Engineers in the South Florida Water Management District.

v   And has many more homeless people than you might

have thought.

vi   This linguistic gymnastics is a large part of my reason for writing *Fake Diseases*, just to clarify with our audience how we must speak about health problems under the foot of our Big Brother.

vii   If we were more informed about fish *farming* practices, we would probably also demand better.

viii   There is a similar concept with population. Government propaganda has us believing that there are "too many people" on Earth, and that this is a huge problem. Yet, since government performance is judged by GDP, governments all over the world actively import more people. More people means better GDP and more taxes, but has absolutely nothing to do with the wellbeing of the people or the environment.

ix   Unfortunately, Musk's SpaceX was recently awarded nearly 900 million dollars in federal subsidies.

x   The book *Freakonomics*, by Steven Levitt has an excellent chapter called *Why Do Drug Dealers Still Live with Their Moms?*

xi   I could almost say this was a positive action from government, but I would also ask the reader to consider the fact that our ignorance about drugs, and the resulting pharmaceutical industry, is largely only in existence because of a hundred-plus-year-old monopoly, wholly supported by the government since the Flexner Report in 1910.

xii   As with the speeding tickets, I do have several friends who have been criminally charged with this "vandalism." I actually have one friend who was indeed deterred from further illegal painting after he was caught. Interestingly, this had nothing to do with the police – his dad threatened him heavily, and it worked. My friend respected his father and believed his threats.

xiii   Unless they subscribe to Zionism.

xiv   In Canada and other countries, media stations are required to air a certain percentage of content produced in the country. I think we do not need the government to ensure "Canadian content". If we want to see Canadian-specific or Australian-specific content, media companies can respond to our market demand.

www.ingramcontent.com/pod-product-compliance
Lightning Source LLC
Chambersburg PA
CBHW051052250726
48656CB00001B/277